THE HEARTBREAK MENDER 2

GEORGE PANTAGES

George Pantages Ministries

Copyright © 2019

The Heartbreak Mender 2

By George Pantages

Printed in the United States of America

ISBN 978-0-9989538-4-7

All rights reserved solely by the authors. The authors guarantee all contents are original and do not infringe upon the legal rights of any other person or work. No part of this book may be reproduced in any form without the permission of the authors.

Unless stated otherwise, all Scripture references come from the NKJV translation of the Bible, copyright © 2006 Thomas Nelson.

KJV. Copyright © 2006 by Thomas Nelson.

George Pantages Ministries

Cell 512 785-6324
geopanjr@yahoo.com
Georgepantages.com

TABLE OF CONTENTS

Chapter 1
Nora Casas
What to do when chronic disease takes over your life............ 11

Chapter 2
Stephanie Pantages
Depression led me to attempted suicide................................ 25

Chapter 3
Samantha Marin
As a baby I was handicapped but not crippled...................... 39

Chapter 4
Isabel Clavesilla
My suffering led me to a life of intercessory prayer 55

Chapter 5
Unique Arreaga
I had to deal with cancer at the age of fifteen........................ 67

Chapter 6
Renie Madrid
When life threatening accidents happen, God has the final say .. 83

Chapter 7
Esther Zazueta
I overcame cancer 91

Chapter 8
Daniel & Jasmin Torres
Our marriage was saved when our baby almost died............ 101

Chapter 9
Andrew & Tamara Goodwin
Two years old is too young to die 117

Chapter 10
Diana Cardenas
Brokenness was my training ground for ministry................. 129

Pastor Rodolfo & Martha Guía

DEDICATION

About 11 years ago we took a great step of faith to leave California to live in Texas. The Longhorn state, in my prayers appeared to be where God wanted us. It was somewhat of a bold move because we had no family or friends in Texas. When we finally settled on Cedar Park (just outside of Austin) we were very comfortable with our decision. It was at that time a change in how we do ministry came about. Instead of waiting for Pastors to initiate an invitation, the Lord asked me to take the initiative and began to call pastors in the area. Terrified as I was to be calling men of God I did not know and even worse they didn't know me, I called one particular pastor who has since then been a great help to our ministry. He not only opened the doors to his church, but he also took the time to recommend me to other pastors in the area so I could establish myself.

To this day, we still minister in his church, although many of his members are freaked out by how the Lord moves when I minister. His continued help is so appreciated but I honestly can say his friendship is even more valuable. Again, thank you pastor and sis. Guia for all you have done for us.

APPRECIATION

I would like to take the time to appreciate the following people for their contribution on the publication of this book:

    Michelle Levigne – Editor
    Mlevigne.com

    Luis Villegas – Book Cover Design
    illuistrations@gmail.com

    Dalila Janos – Spanish Translation

    Maria Pantages – Typesetting

Your professionalism and expertise rang true throughout the entire process, making my writing a whole lot better than it really is.

Nora Casas

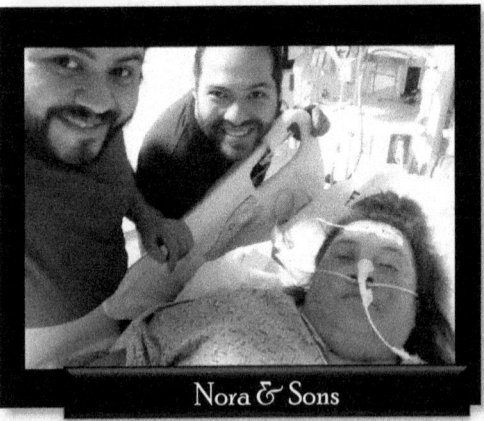
Nora & Sons

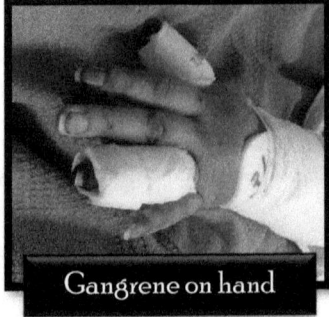
Gangrene on hand

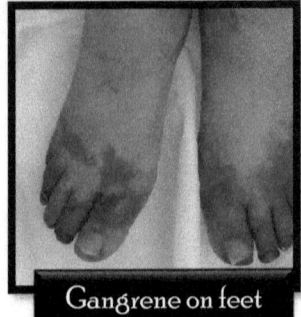
Gangrene on feet

CHAPTER 1

Nora Casas

Keeping yourself virtuous till marriage for that "happily ever after" experience, fell way short of my expectations. Early on, I realized that something was wrong after the knot was tied. I didn't quite know in the beginning what took my husband's attention, but there were signs that scared me half to death. It was just past the honeymoon stage and he had become distant and preoccupied with not only ministry, but more so on himself. He was unable to form an intimate relationship or provide the soul deep companionship that I craved. Nothing seemed to spark a flame in our relationship, and I just could not figure it out. At times I slaved over a hot stove, believing what I was going to serve him would not only please him but open him up to some romance later that evening. That old adage, "the way to a man's heart is through his stomach," did not work for me. When he came home, the table was set, candles were lit, but to no avail. I brought this to his attention, but it fell on deaf ears. He began to let himself go physically, and little by little lovemaking became less frequent and less interesting.

In the beginning, like all newlyweds, I overlooked the defects and the shortcomings because I felt and believed that the "good stuff" outweighed the bad and that everything would be okay. A lifelong commitment was what I signed up for and never in my wildest imagination did I think it would be this way. For whatever reason, I ignored all the warning signs.

I was young and soon with child when the next reality check presented itself. I had to go out and work to supplement our income to make ends meet and soon realized that life in ministry entailed a great deal of sacrifice, mostly on my part. My marriage did not slowly erode and starve to death, my marriage was damaged early on when I realized I had married a man addicted to porn, who kept it a secret. To my horror, I caught him on porn sites, which devastated me. Every dream I had in our marriage was shattered by hidden sexual sin. Looking back on it now, it all made sense how dysfunctional he was. Mistrust consumed my every thought and I hated the sin that took all his attention. I was so hurt and ashamed of our life. It was not easy for me because I felt I couldn't expose my husband, who was a pastor, father, and the son of a well-known dignitary of our church organization. I felt I just had to deal with it. My marriage was controlled by a pornography addiction that he could not overcome, which eventually caused it to crumble! Sad to say, it was a sin that affected my faith in God as well. Faced with horrific acts of betrayal, I slowly began to walk away from God, blaming Him for permitting this mess. The hypocrisy I felt a part of, the pressure to pretend I had my life all together, was all a big hoax. It was just too much for me to handle. No one likes to be exposed and no one was there to help me navigate through these troubled waters. In the end, we separated, which eventually led to divorce. And worst of all, no one seemed to care. My world was sad, depressed, lonely and I was so angry that I walked away from God as well, thinking I was getting even with Him, but actually I was falling more and more into darkness. I no longer had a cry in my heart for Him. I felt victimized and sin drew me further and further from God. I also blamed the world for my miserable life and all the things that overwhelmed me. I struggled through life hurt and resentful and couldn't get past the memory of my loneliness in my marriage.

    I was so despondent that I started to see patterns of toxic behavior that would shortly affect me physically. In my depression, I turned to food for comfort, and overeating became an obsession. Addictive eating was a self-destructive behavior that would later destroy my health, as you will soon read the traumatic, almost unreal circumstances I faced. This addiction almost took my life. I hated the sin that consumed both of our lives, yet it was my sin that almost killed me, literally!

    Eighteen years later, I was so lost and far from God. My life became spiritually dead. I didn't talk to God in prayer and didn't listen to what He had to say in His Word. I stopped reading my Bible. I struggled so hard to get back, a struggle I knew the devil would not easily give up. It actually took an experience with demons in my home for me to realize I needed deliverance from the devil who wanted my soul. I'll never forget the ugly feeling I got when I felt this presence in my room that put a chill up my spine and hair standing up on my arms, not letting me sleep. All night I clutched my Bible for protection, believing that doing so I could escape all the drama in my life at that time finally falling asleep. At times I would read the Bible all night, asking God to forgive me. I remember trying my hardest to reach God after many years of darkness and shame, I felt that I had betrayed God. That night I was awaken by an "angel's" presence that embraced me with such a soothing feeling of protection! The loving, sweet feeling God gave me let me know that no matter what situation I was in, He had forgiven me and had my back.

It wasn't long before my faith was tested again, and He chose me to experience this chronic condition. I don't know all His purpose in this, but I think part of the reason is to teach me some of His principles for living which brings Him glory, bless me, and build my faith even stronger to stand no matter what comes my way...

The day I was informed I was in kidney failure, I was sick with what I thought was bronchitis. Weeks passed, and even with antibiotics I still was not any better. The doctor told me, "Sorry, but you need to be hospitalized." I called my brother who also was my pastor. He shocked me with what he said! He told me God was putting me through something to test my faith. I immediately fell in the elevator, yelling, "No, not me. God why?" Doctors said once they put a catheter in me, then they would proceed with dialysis, and of course they promised I would feel 100 percent better. I did not know that it would be a death sentence. Not only did I have a difficult time adjusting, but complications seemed to always haunt me. Over the years, problems such as bone disease, high blood pressure, nerve damage, and anemia racked my body. Thirteen years dealing with chronic illness have been a long and painful journey. So many doctors to deal with, unending treatments, constant hospitalizations, all the while pushing my endurance to its limits. I can't even begin to tell you how hard it was for me. Treatments three times a week without fail. No guarantees that I would get any better. Complications from veins collapsing and infections, all which overwhelmed me each time! Gradually my health declined, and I started to face even more bad news. A decade of deep suffering with chronic illness was a life I never was prepared for. This was way too much for me to bear, way too much for me to comprehend, and it would forever change my life! The only way I could ever survive was through my faith in Him. Some days more difficult than others, each day has been a challenge. Feeling alone to ponder unaddressed questions, and emotions. So many tests, so many medications, so many different diagnoses. When would it ever end?

I found out next that I had Antiphospholipid syndrome. This is (an immune disorder in which abnormal antibodies are linked to abnormal blood clots in veins and arteries, which could cause strokes.) There is no cure for this disease. A blood clot on my right leg caused me to sleep in a recliner for over a year, and fear came over me worried this clot would travel to my heart or brain.

My platelets became a challenge and I had to see an oncologist/endocrinologist. My levels were so low, forcing another hospital stay. While there, I was told I could possibly bleed to death. I then went through spinal tests for bone marrow, with the possibility of having leukemia. Wow, what would I do then? So scared! I felt I needed to learn all I could to coordinate my care, not always trusting what the doctors had to say. This became very important for me, so I could stand and trust in God to see me through.

I chose to do home dialysis in 2010 the year my daughter graduated high school. Only days from that 4th of July, I landed in the hospital with pain in my stomach that I couldn't bear. Something was really wrong, and I discovered I had "peritonitis". It was a serious condition that needed immediate medical attention. Prompt intravenous antibiotics were needed to treat the infection. Surgery is sometimes necessary to remove infected tissue. The infection can spread and become life-threatening if it isn't treated promptly. I was placed on life support, because of bacterial infection with sepsis (harmful microorganisms in the blood, leading to the malfunctioning of organs, shock, or death) throughout my whole body. The doctors opened up my stomach and removed the catheter for the dialysis. My stomach was left open to heal and close up on its own. Days turned to weeks, weeks turned to months, and they didn't think I would make it. My colon, now with a hole in it, caused even more trouble. The doctors muttered even more devastating news, in that I possibly would need a "colostomy." It's a surgical procedure that brings one end of the large intestine out through an opening (stoma) made in the abdominal wall. Stools moving through the intestine drain through the stoma into a bag attached to the abdomen. I spoke with my surgeon and he told me the colon could possibly heal! I put my trust in God and elected for a long journey for recovery! I had spent months in the hospital and felt so alone. I remember praying to the Lord that I couldn't do this alone, so please send visitors to encourage me. Because I was going through so much pain, they gave me intravenous pain medication called dilaudid, a narcotic, which I became addicted to. I had difficulty focusing, irritability, sadness, and I felt my body wanting more before I reached the four-hour point, I also wanted more to get high. I recognized I was dependent on pain medication and did not want to leave the hospital a drug addict. I asked my pastor to come and pray for me, and from that day on I refused any pain medication, completely depending on God.

Diverticulitis caused a rupture, spilling intestinal waste into my abdominal cavity. Two surgical suction balls were hung from my stomach to pump the fluid mixed with feces. I dealt with wound vac nurses and home care daily. Where was my life leading me? The word HEALING impressed my heart, and suddenly my faith in God grew strong, hoping that God would heal my colon and return it to normal. Through the 3 ½ months of my hospital stay, God answered my prayers. Each day I had a visitor and my colon healed after eight to ten months.

Sometimes I couldn't find the will to go on, the motivation to see it through. Often I felt people assumed I was being punished and couldn't be used by God because of my illness and sin, but that's what the devil wanted me to believe. I became an over-thinker and a worrier, spending many sleepless nights wondering "if God really did love me". I felt afflicted many times by people who made me feel I didn't have enough faith to be healed. They made me feel like I had done something wrong. What was worse was I felt God was disappointed in me. I've cried more tears than I can keep track of. Pain consumed my body and all I knew was it was too much to bear! I began to feel the strain of being debilitated. Yet God holds all my tears. This I know for sure (Psalm 56:8). Being judgmental does not help and makes the person being judged feel alienated and more alone. Forgive those who fail you, whether friends, family, or even your church family. Forgive and move on.

My spleen was then removed, and now I have to be careful because the spleen provides defense against viruses and pneumonia. Just my luck, one in a thousand get affected and that one was me. By the time I knew that I was sick with pneumonia but the nurses didn't pay attention to my complaint of chills. They told me I had no other symptoms to do a culture. After days of complaining, to the point I had chills all night, I called my nephrologist at three in the morning. He told me to go straight to the ER. I went to dialysis instead, and when I got back home, I didn't even have the strength to get out of my car. My neighbors helped me out of the car. I dreaded the thought of going back to the hospital but I knew I had to go. When you've been in the hospital as much as I have, that makes it harder to want to be hospitalized. My son took me in and immediately they took me to an exam room. The pneumonia was already septic, a life-threatening state. They did test after test, and I was told I was going to have to be put on twenty-four hour dialysis. They placed a catheter. I could not move my leg or I could die, was how the nurse put it to me. I can't describe to you the face of that nurse. She looked demonic, and fear came over me. I felt my life was in danger.

I called for my pastor, but he was out of town. I then called my nephew, but he was at work and couldn't get to the hospital. He said "Tia, you have the glory of God with your uncut hair." That was when I asked my son to pull down my hair. I pleaded in the name of Jesus, "Holy are you, Lord! Send your ministering angels of protection around me." Just as I mentioned the name of JESUS, I began to speak in tongues, and lo and behold, the presence of three angels appeared, one on each side of me and one at my feet. My tongues turned to laughter, then I told my son "they are here and I'll be okay." My son told me my countenance changed from a pale yellow to a soft pink!

From that point on I was placed on five days around the clock dialysis and seven days of life support. My family was called in and told there was only 1 percent chance of survival and did not give them much hope that I would make it. Family came in from out of town, church members travailed around the clock for me, and I was placed on a national prayer list during this time. While on life-support, I saw visions of people lost and consumed with Snapchat, and inappropriate pictures being posted and shared. In my seven days, I remember hearing the voice of the Lord, audible in my ears, telling me, "Tell my people I come soon, keep my commandments." I remember struggling with the nurse, tugging and fighting, pulling, and then I was awakened after seven days. I had bruising on my wrist where in my vision I was struggling with the nurse. I later found out I had tried pulling the tubing from my mouth, so my hands were restrained and tied down. To my astonishment, both my hands and feet were black and blue from cut off blood circulation, and gangrene had set in. Before I knew it, my feet became necrotic and doctors had talked to the family about amputation of my feet and hands. As soon as I realized my state, I "could not" and "would not" accept this. I started with my hands, squeezing a ball, helping the blood to circulate to my hand. A long battle was ahead, but nothing was going to keep me down. Right now, all I thought of was to fight, and God miraculously moved on my behalf and now all I heard was "Be still and know that I am God." After ten months bed-ridden, my toes were completely necrotic and mummified. Well, all I had right now was to be still. With daily nurse wound care and the risk of infection looming, I couldn't accept losing my toes. The day one fell off on its own, it was so hard to see and very painful to try to walk. Thanks to being bed-ridden and convalescing in pain, the desire to live on was slowly dying. I had a feeling of worthlessness and didn't want to face life in a wheelchair, nor did I want to depend on or be a burden on family or friends. I had tears at night, wailing at all hours. My daughter would come out and ask me if I was okay. "NO, I wish you would have just let me die." In this place of darkness, I just didn't want to continue. I got myself to church every Sunday and pushed myself. Even going through this incessant heaviness, His glory emanated miraculously! I danced and praised the Lord through this difficult time. The decision to have the remaining toes amputated came next. At times, the devil would put in my mind that if I had not danced or walked, maybe I wouldn't have made it worse on my feet and I wouldn't have lost my toes.

Wow, all the shoes I had meticulously matched with every one of my outfits were useless. I gave most of them away, and in the end I discarded the rest. No more open-toe shoes, no more pedicures, no more heels. The process was overwhelming and emotional. I had to wear therapeutic shoes with Velcro. So blah! Material things that you take for granted, once taken away, you realize they had consumed your life more than they should have.

After the first surgery, I had two-and-a-half toes left. I was deformed and tried holding on to balance so I could walk, without being in a wheelchair or walker. So much pain. I took Norco every four hours just to mask the pain, waddling around and feeling so helpless. God was with me through it all. I literally could not move with the chance of infection and gangrene setting in. When a second surgery removed the last two-and-a-half toes, my brother teased me and called me "two-toe." I had compromised my health by not having my toes amputated early on, and I went through ten months of nurse care and wound care, only to have them all amputated in the end. I realized people died from gangrene and knew that God loved me so much that with all I had lost, I still had the breath of life. For that I was truly grateful. Through each step, I could see God's goodness and I embraced my sickness, suffering, and trials with grace. We can then grow in virtue, and dwell in His love. Chronic illness can be a burden, but the glory of God shines even when my body feels like I cannot go on. There is constant pain, and I have a restricted diet I must abide by to avoid other complications. My body is usually too tired to push through the day without a nap. I'm generally dizzy, nauseous, and, fatigued, with loss of appetite, weakness, sleep problems, muscle twitches and cramps, persistent itching, and chest pain if fluid builds up around the lining of my heart. This includes shortness of breath if fluid builds up in the lungs, anemia, weak bones and increased risk of bone fracture.

    I have a decreased immune response, which makes me more vulnerable to infections. I've missed social occasions and rarely get invited, so I stay home alone, managing my pain or resting my fatigued body, always seeing God throughout it all. Chronic illness is accompanied by constant suffering, but it is also met with constant joy. God is my comforter and brings me joy.

    Being on my deathbed has made me take a good look in the mirror. I am so grateful God gave me a second and third chance. I really needed a check-up from how I lived.

The Heartbreak Mender 2

I have been able to see people with their toxic relationships destroying their marriages, believing now that I could be some help to them. On the other hand, for those who struggle with chronic illnesses, I can share with them that no matter what comes their way, God is always faithful! Making time for God through every situation is what got me closer. The days and nights I cried, His presence always met me with such love.

Just recently, I was faced with yet another trial, only this time I'm in shock, no talking or praying to God. You see, I've been doing the work-up for my kidney transplant. I was denied twice in the past for obesity. Ten years later, I've lost 110 pounds, so they can't possibly deny me now, "right?" Wrong. After doing an ultrasound of my heart, they discovered something. I've been walking and eating right, so how can this be? I am now doing another test TEE (transesophageal echocardiogram). It is a special probe containing an ultrasound transducer at its tip and is passed into the patient's esophagus, allowing image and Doppler evaluation, which can be recorded, making detailed pictures of my heart and the arteries that lead to and from it. The nurse told me, "We're doing this test because we found a mass in your heart, a right atrial mass to be exact." I let go of all my emotions and couldn't stop crying. The results weren't good -- "weak heart muscle" -- and infraction levels at 25 percent. My social worker informed me they couldn't do a kidney transplant and I needed to see a heart specialist for possible open-heart surgery. "Lord, deliver me and help me to be an overcomer." I asked Him to remove all fear and I placed my heart in His hands. A repeat test showed the infraction levels at 45 percent, and the doctor did not think I needed open heart surgery. God has always been in control, even when we may doubt along the way. He has always been faithful and has always brought victory into my life.

At some point, my emotions subsided and I faced my new reality. I'm no longer the person I used to be, although chronic illness has robbed me of so much. My physical deficiencies have limited me, but did not stop me from being determined to share my gifts and talents with other ladies. I volunteer at a senior center, teaching crochet, sewing, and needle point. Volunteering builds self-confidence and contributes to feelings of value and self-worth. It helps to overcome social isolation.

God has transformed my world by sharing comfort, hope, and support to those who are suffering. Helping others to gain perspective and build meaningful purpose in their lives is my new mission in life. Christ's sacrifice gives us perfect hope, not to mention help in both the good and in the bad times. Hallelujah!!!

Contac information for speaking engagements: Norahanddesign@yahoo.com

Stephanie Pantages

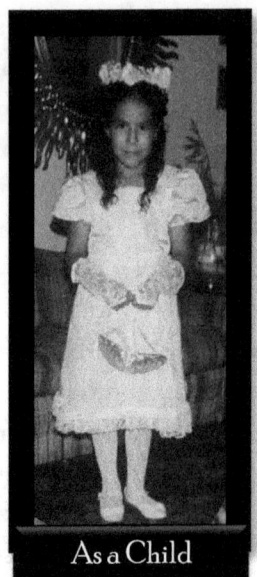
As a Child

Rancho Cucamonga Home

CHAPTER 2

Stephanie Pantages

When we are young, we dream of all that we will become. We make plans for our lives and expect everything to turn out the way we hope it will. What we are rarely told is that failure is going to be a large part of the process, and more times than not it is in those failures that we become who we are destined to be. Pain oftentimes is partnered with our purpose. It is easy to get lost in the expectations of what our lives should look like once we reach a certain age. When that doesn't happen, we wonder where we went wrong. When my father asked me to write a chapter for this book, I responded with laughter. I thought he was joking, because I had just expressed to him how lost I felt. I am in my thirties, and I feel like a failure. I know we aren't supposed to compare ourselves to others because comparison is the thief of joy, but I am here to be honest about my struggles and hopefully in some way you can relate. I asked the Lord what I should write about and why my story mattered. I kept hearing, your story isn't one of punishment but of preparation for your purpose. Pain must be felt, tears must fall. It is time to stop running away from Me. There is one thing that I am sure of, and that is every person reading this book knows the pain of heartbreak. It comes in many forms and more than likely it happens in ways you would not expect and from the people you trust most. I have spent countless nights crying out to God, asking Him to let me die. The majority of my life has been spent running away from the Lord because I was afraid to trust His plans. It was only recently that the Lord showed me pain hidden deep in my heart that has kept me in toxic cycles I have been unable to break away from. It astounds me how God will give you a way out when He knows you are about to go too far. Unbeknownst to me, this past November my father and stepmother came to California to visit family. I happened to run into them at one of our favorite burger joints and I knew God was giving me a way to confess in order to repent of the things I had been doing. I fought the Lord's conviction while I sat with them as they finished their meal. I knew my father could feel something was off with me, but I kept my mouth shut. A day or two passed and I humbled myself, called my dad, and asked if we could meet so we could talk. He suggested we grab a bite to eat and I agreed.

Although I have always had a special relationship with my father, I can't recall ever talking to him about what I went through during my parents' separation and divorce. It was almost as if I had two childhoods. One was filled with wonderful memories of my father taking us to the park of our choosing every Saturday. Going to the public library, where I would play hopscotch on the huge carpet in the children's area. I remember my father being the one to teach me how to ride a bike and how to tie my shoelaces. When I was five years old, I would hear him get ready for work and he would be singing or whistling. Now that I am older, I find myself singing and whistling just like my dad. I also have the most nicknames out of my siblings, and I love how I have my own special song. My dad is in a lot of my most treasured memories. Maybe in some ways I was trying to protect the happy memories by keeping the dark side of my childhood a secret from him. I had to choose to trust him with my pain to enable what I was about to confess to make sense. You see, for as long as I can remember, my mother and I have had a tense and complicated relationship. I am one of three children. I am the middle child. My mother would joke that if I had been born first, she might not have had more children. In her defense, my older brother was a well-behaved, quiet child, and I was the opposite. I was independent, energetic, and a curious child. I was a lot to handle, and there were times when my mother was verbally and physically abusive towards me. For those of you who don't know my mother, trust me when I say that she was and is gorgeous. I wanted to look like her, and I felt as if I was a disappointment because I didn't quite measure up. She has a petite figure, and when I was younger she had long, beautiful, straight hair. I was born with curly hair, a curvy figure, and I was taller than her by the time I was eleven years old. My mother would criticize me about my weight, and I remember reading a comment she made in my baby book saying I was chubby when I was just five years old. I am not sure when it began, but I started to use food as a coping mechanism. I remember being eight years old when my mother found empty fruit snack wrappers hidden under my dresser. Her reaction terrified me, so I ran out of my room, past my dad in the living room, and out our front door. I ran in the dark for a couple of miles and eventually made my way back home. As I turned the corner onto our street, I saw my dad at the end of our driveway with his head down. He looked so sad and I wanted to tell him, I wanted to trust him, but I was afraid that he would take my mom's side and it would make things worse, so I kept the abuse to myself. I was blessed to grow up on the same street as my grandmother Amelia and my papa Leo, so whenever the abuse from my mother began to be too much, I would go to their house to feel loved and safe again.

My grandmother was incredibly kind, and she made me feel secure, worthy, and like I wasn't too hard to love. Whenever I would get in trouble, I didn't fear her but respected the fact that she would explain to me why what I did was wrong. She let me ask questions and made me feel what I had to say was important. Looking back, I feel as if I gravitated towards my dad because he and my grandmother had similar personalities. In the summer of my thirteenth year, we moved from Pico Rivera, CA, to Rancho Cucamonga, CA, due to my dad's job being relocated. I hated it. To make matters worse, it wasn't long until my dad chose to quit his job to evangelize full time. At this point in telling my dad my story, I began to cry because I knew that I had to share with him the details of how I decided to attempt suicide for the first time. He knew I had tried, but I never went into detail about how I did it. I was now fifteen years old and being without my grandmother and dad, my mother's abuse became too much and I wanted the pain to end. I remember getting in a fight with my mother while my dad was out of state, preaching. When he got home, he asked me how my weekend was, because God had told him I was in trouble and he needed to pray for me. I cried and told him how my mom was constantly commenting about my weight and how she made me feel worthless. I didn't tell him that I took a bottle of pills, hoping that I would fall asleep and never wake up. My dad offered to help by going on walks and work our way up to jogging. It helped, but it was temporary, because he began to evangelize more frequently and would be gone for longer periods of time. I tried a couple of more times to take my life, each time consuming more and more pills, not understanding why God wouldn't let me die. It was almost as if He would pump my stomach of the pills, and no matter how many I took, all I ended up doing was throwing up the entire night. So eventually I gave up. At this point while explaining my story to my dad, I started to cry because I knew the most difficult memories were about to be shared.

When God opened the door for me to move back to California from Texas, I was irritated with Him for bringing me back to the city where my life fell apart. I currently live less than four miles from the last home we lived in together as a family. When I arrived in Rancho Cucamonga in late April of 2018, I drove by my old house and I saw my old bedroom window. I sat there staring at the house and cried in my car while the memories ran through my mind, and each one was more painful than the last. I asked God why He was doing this to me. Why was He torturing me? It was all too much, and I begged Him to stop. A memory of me at fifteen years old flashed through my mind. I had been playing with our next door neighbor in her backyard, and I rolled my left ankle so badly that I couldn't walk. My sister ran over to our house, and my brother and dad helped me into our family car so that I could go to the hospital. I was supposed to go jogging with my dad that evening, and my mother accused me of hurting myself on purpose so that I wouldn't have to work out with him. I stared at her in shock. How could she think I would do this to myself? I sprained my ankle so badly that I had to use crutches for a couple of weeks. As I continued to cry, the next memory ran through my mind. I remembered the day my best friend, Tina came over to pick me up so that I could spend the night at her house. An hour before she came over, my mother had driven me to work and took this opportunity to tell me that she and my dad were separating and she didn't want me. She didn't care that I was in the middle of my senior year of high school. The thought of moving was unbearable. As I got out of the car and walked up to the door, her words kept repeating in my mind. She didn't want me. As I entered the building, I could feel the hot tears fall from my eyes. My manager came up to me and asked what was wrong. I couldn't speak. All I could do was sob uncontrollably, and after a couple of minutes I was able to tell her what had transpired between my mother and me in the car on the way to work. My manager was kind enough to allow me to go home. The next thing I remember is my best friend sitting next to me on my front steps while I cried. We eventually left my house and went to hers, and the last thing I remember was dropping my overnight bag on her bedroom floor and crying on her bed. It was the first time I had felt my heart break. It physically hurt me, and I felt as if I was dying. I felt completely worthless, rejected, unloved, abandoned, broken and confused. How could someone who brought me into this world say such things without considering how her words would affect me? I truly hated her. She broke my trust for the last time, and at seventeen years old I made peace with the fact that this woman would never change. I was done with her. Our relationship wouldn't be repaired until I was almost thirty years old, but I will get into that a little bit later. The last memory began to run through my mind, and it was the last day I spent in our home. I remembered every detail, and all of a sudden I was closing my bedroom door and I locked it so that I could be alone. I looked around my empty room and then I fell to the floor and cried bitter tears while burying my face in my carpet. I knew nothing was ever going to be the same again, and it was in that moment that I told God that I wanted nothing to do with Him or His plans for my life. I blamed God for breaking up my family, because He was the one who made my dad an evangelist, knowing it would take him away from us for long periods of time. I graduated from high school earlier in the month, and instead of hope for my future I felt fear and anger. I was hurt that my dad and brother had left me alone to endure living alone with my mother and sister. It wasn't until I moved up to Modesto two years later that I was able to forgive them, because I saw how they were struggling just as I was.

 In the first year after my parents separated, my mother, little sister and I moved around a lot. My sister had recently started her freshman year of high school and I did my best to be there for her. I lovingly nicknamed her Kid, because my mother wasn't around much, so I felt as if I had to try to fill my mother's place. My parents married when they were twenty-one years old, and after twenty-five years of marriage, my mother was finally able to experience freedom to do whatever she wanted. Eventually she fell in love with a man who wasn't kind to my sister and me. We didn't understand why she was choosing him over us. When I was almost twenty years old, I asked my dad if I could move up north with him and my brother, because I knew that I was on the verge of attempting suicide again. I explained that my mother and I were constantly fighting, and although I had never been physically abusive towards her, I came close once when she kept coming at me. Thankfully my sister told my mother to back off and to get out of our room, and we sat there and cried. I told my sister that I had to leave her, and I felt like a disappointment because I wanted to be there for her, but it was too much for me. The little girl I used to be, who was overflowing with joy, was dying, and I wasn't ready to give her up. The next couple of years of my life are a blur. My relationship with God was nonexistent, and all the dreams and plans I had for my life didn't matter anymore. I felt like I had lost my purpose and that everything I was taught while growing up in the church was all a lie. I felt as if God didn't love me, so I wasn't going to waste my time loving Him. The spirit of rejection gripped my heart and mind, and I allowed the pain to change me. I accepted the lies that the devil had been telling me for the majority of my life, and although I was able to fight against further suicide attempts, I wasn't exactly alive either.

  When I was twenty-two years old, I fell in love for the first time. We were friends first and we met at work and it was completely unexpected. At the time I was living with my dad and brother in Arcadia, CA, and when I began to rebel against my dad and his rules, he kicked me out. My mother wouldn't allow me to move back in with her, so my cousin Melissa said I could come and live with her while I figured things out. Feeling abandoned and misunderstood by my parents only deepened the bond between my boyfriend Carter and me. Two months after my dad kicked me out, my grandmother Amelia passed away, six months after suffering a stroke. This was due to complications from an angioplasty procedure she had done without telling us, because she didn't want us to worry about her. I couldn't take the pain of losing her, because she was more of a mother to me than my mom was. My anger towards the Lord increased and my longing to feel safe and loved caused me to decide to move in with Carter. We were together for almost three years, and when we broke up the spirit of rejection grew stronger. My dad had remarried and decided to move to Texas. I asked to go with him because I needed a fresh start. In truth, I was running away from the pain. I had never been to Texas and I knew it was going to be difficult, but I never expected it to be as hard as it was. My dad and Maria continued to evangelize full time, so that meant they were gone for months on end. That made it easier for me to hide my depression from everyone. I got to the point where I wasn't leaving the apartment and I was unable to sleep. I eventually got help and started to see a therapist and started taking antidepressants and sleeping pills. I was on them for about seven months, and three months after I had been off of medication I moved in with my mother and my stepdad, who were living in Colorado. I pursued a career in the healthcare industry. I thought that was the main reason God led me there, but during the year-and-a-half I spent with my mother, our relationship was repaired. It was difficult in the beginning and we fought quite a bit. Over time, we would have deep conversations and she shared with me how my grandmother was physically and verbally abusive to her. My heart broke as she began to cry and tell me what her childhood was like, and for the first time I felt empathy for her. She grew up in a large family and she had to work at a young age to contribute to her family's wellbeing. All this time, I had thought that my mom was cold and cruel when she was actually in pain like I had been. She didn't know how to deal with what her parents did to her. With my dad being busy with the church, she was left alone a lot, so she was overwhelmed. My mom also shared how my grandmother was abused, and it was then that I realized it was a sort of generational curse. I knew it had to end with me. She and my stepdad ended up moving to Texas and I stayed in Colorado for another six months before moving back to Texas with my dad and Maria in the fall of 2015. I remember crying on the phone, telling them how lost I felt and how frustrated I was with myself for not being able to move forward. I hated myself for not living up to my potential. I didn't understand why God kept tugging at my heart asking me to come back to Him. All I did was disappoint Him. Then my dad told me that we can't disappoint God, because when you disappoint someone it means that your actions surprised them and God already knew what I was going to do before I did it.

    I made the move back to Texas and stayed for two-and-a-half years before coming back to California in the spring of last year. The transition has been uncomfortable, lonely, and painful, but it has allowed me to be honest with myself about what has been holding me back. I was tired of running in circles. I wanted to move forward, and I wanted to be free from the weight of my pain. I started to give up on myself. The devil taunted me for trying to repair my relationship with God, because I had tried many times in the past and the result was always the same. I would eventually retreat to my toxic coping mechanisms. I was infuriated with myself for not being able to move forward and thought that maybe the prophesy spoken over my life were incorrect because I kept making the same mistakes, yet expecting to have different results. I thought God had given up on me because I couldn't seem to get things right. Over the last four years, I allowed the devil to use fear to cause me to compromise myself and settle for men who were not what I wanted in a husband. I knew that I deserved more than what I was settling for, but I told my dad how terrified I was to give in to God, because I watched his ministry grow while our family fell apart. What if I allowed myself to wait for the type of godly husband I wanted, just to have him divorce me because he couldn't handle the call that God had for my life? I figured if I settled for a husband who was less than I deserved, then when he left me it would hurt less because I could remind myself that he wasn't what I wanted anyway. I didn't feel worthy to wait on God to give me a godly marriage, so I tried to make things happen on my own. I was getting older and I desperately wanted to have children. The devil would tell me that I had to take matters into my own hands, because by the time I finally fully committed to Christ it would be too late, so I might as well pick a man who was close enough to what I wanted in a spouse and worry about the consequences later.

 As I finished confessing to my father, he comforted me and we finished our meal and went our separate ways. A day or two later, he called me and said that the Lord told him to tell me not to worry about having children, because when I got married, I would get pregnant almost immediately. The Lord has never said anything like that to me, and I love Him for allowing me to cling to this promise while I allow Him to make my heart new again. I know that some of you may feel that God has forgotten you and you have lost hope in ever becoming free from whatever is weighing you down. If you don't remember anything I have written up to this point, I need you to remember the next few sentences. I too felt as if God had forgotten me. I had dug myself into a grave that I could not see a way out of. I understand how you feel when you are crying in the middle of the night, asking God to take your life so that you can be at peace. My story is only beginning, but in the midst of the chaos and confusion, I am choosing to trust in Him. I will no longer agree with the lies that say I am destined to remain in this vicious cycle of depression, mistrust, rejection, fear and abandonment. The Lord has given each of us all that we need to break free, but we also have to remember that we have to engage in the battle for our souls. We can't continue the same cycles, expecting God to honor our disobedience. I can assure you, He did not honor mine. There will be times when you will be lonely, because I have felt the same way during this process of becoming and you will make mistakes just as I have. That's okay, but you need to get back up and continue to move forward. You need to let go of the past and remind yourself that even though it may feel like you have been stuck in the same chapter of your life for years, you can no longer live your life this way. Before I ever said I was sorry for all that I've done, He made a way of escape for me, and He has one for you. I am no different from you, I am not more special than you are. God doesn't love me more because my father is an evangelist. We are all the same. I am living proof that God is merciful, loving, and forgiving. At this moment I have more questions than I do answers, and even though I am unsure of how God will use me, or how He will bring my future husband and me together, God is enabling me to trust in Him despite the uncertainties. Nothing is impossible for God, and there's no situation He can't turn around for your good. He took the city where my life fell apart, the city that once held my deepest pain, and made it new again. My once-painful ending has now become a beautiful beginning. I hope that you choose to trust in Him even when it doesn't make sense. You're not alone, and I will be praying for everyone who reads this book. I want you to know that it is possible to have peace and praise God while you wait. Be joyful in hope, because even though my life hasn't turned out how I had planned, He is using my pain for a greater purpose. My best days are not behind me and I am confident in knowing He saved the best for last.

Contac information for speaking engagements:
SLPantages@gmail.com

Samantha Marin

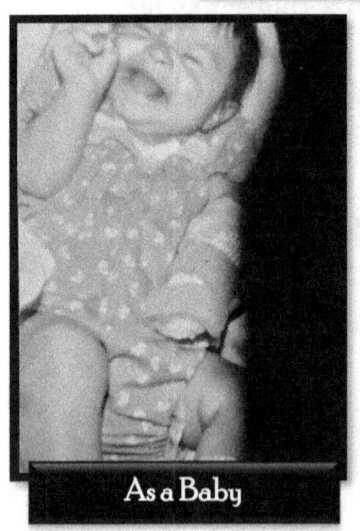

As a Baby

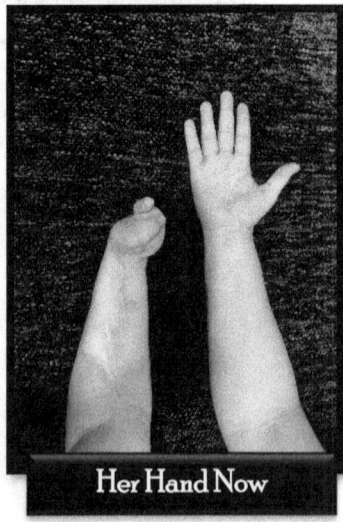

Her Hand Now

CHAPTER 3

Samantha Marin

Now more than ever, I am convinced that God has a plan for every life. He does not make mistakes, and He walks right beside us even before we are fully aware of His presence in our lives. He knows the end from the beginning, and He can take a tragedy and turn it into something beautiful. This is my story.

The Accident

It was a warm June afternoon in 1990. My parents were on their way back from a delivery run in Las Vegas. My dad owned his own trucking company, and he often took my mom along for company on his long trips. When they got back into town, Dad dropped my mom off at the church to pick up their car. She picked up the car and then went to pick up my sister and me from her mom's house. After she picked us up, she went back to the church to meet my dad, who had been waiting there for us in his truck. The plan was for her to follow my dad to the truck yard so he could drop his truck off, and then he would drive us back home in the car. The truck yard was about twenty-five minutes from the church. As they got closer to the yard, my dad pulled on ahead of my mom so he could get to the yard before her. He wanted to park the truck and empty it before she got there. My mom was changing lanes to merge onto the 405 freeway. The last thing she remembers is seeing a big eighteen-wheeler truck merging over into her lane.

Dad arrived at the truck yard, parked the truck, and finished everything he had to do, and then sat and waited for my mom. After some time passed and she did not arrive, he sensed that something was wrong and he decided to get back on the freeway to see if she had gotten a flat tire. He got back onto the freeway, and there was bumper to bumper traffic. He exited and took the street to get onto the freeway going in the opposite direction. As he drove onto the on-ramp, he looked in his rearview mirror and saw our car flipped over, wheels up in the air, spinning. He immediately jammed on the brakes, backed the truck up to the crash site and jumped out of the truck and ran towards the car.

When he got to the car, a highway patrolman tried to stop him from coming any closer. He told the patrolman that his family was in the car involved in the accident and he was immediately allowed through to the crash site. As he came running over, he saw me, a forty-five-day-old baby, lying on the highway surrounded by paramedics. A kneeling lady looked him in the eye and told him, "Don't worry, everything is going to be all right." (Later on, he asked for this same lady, but no one had seen her; he believes with all his heart that she was an angel.) He looked over to see my sister Chanel, not yet two years old, being strapped down on a stretcher with a brace around her neck. My mother was nowhere to be found. When he asked for her, they pointed him toward another ambulance. He looked inside the back of the ambulance and saw my mom lying on a stretcher, covered in blood. He went over to her and tried to talk to her, but she was unresponsive. He continued to try to wake her up. She could not open her eyes, but she could hear him.

He asked, "Lynn, what happened?"

She could hear my sister and me screaming, but she couldn't respond.

He asked her again, "What happened?" and she finally answered, "Where are the girls?" He replied, "They are fine," and he said, "Don't worry, just get a hold of God." She began to pray and then lost consciousness.

My dad tried to ride in the ambulance with her to the hospital, but the highway patrolman told him he could not leave his truck on the highway. He had to drive the truck back to the yard, borrow a car from his boss, and then head to the hospital.

Upon arriving at the hospital, he was told he would have to wait. We were all in critical condition, and the doctors were examining us to figure out just how severe our injuries were. During his time in the waiting room, Dad called his pastor. Our pastor was out of town and could not come to the hospital, but he called members of the church to start a prayer chain. Eventually, a doctor came out to tell my dad that the situation looked very grave and that he might be "going home alone" because his family would probably not survive. When the accident took place, the impact of the crash was so powerful that it had ejected my mother and sister from the vehicle. The doctor told Dad that his wife was in a coma and unresponsive. His oldest daughter, Chanel, had a broken neck, and the baby (me) was in critical condition. The impact of the crash had caused the vehicle to flip over several times. I was still strapped into my car seat, and as the vehicle flipped over several times, my left arm was smashed over and over again. My elbow got pushed up into my shoulder, and my fingers were mangled and completely black. The surgeons had a meeting for several hours to determine how to handle my surgery. It would be very complicated and dangerous because I was so small.

After the doctor talked to my dad, he had to wait again and was still not allowed to see us. While he was waiting, the assistant pastor showed up, and they began praying for us in the waiting room. After some time, they were allowed to visit my mom's hospital room, but she was completely unresponsive. My dad and the assistant pastor prayed for her and then went to visit Chanel in her hospital room next. When they entered Chanel's room, the nurses told him not to move her because she had on a neck brace and was still strapped to a board because her neck was broken. The nurses loosened the straps so that she could be prayed for on her head, and the assistant pastor and Dad prayed for her. As they finished praying for her and began to lift their hands away from her, she was healed instantly and immediately sat up. The nurses were shocked. They called the doctor in to check on her, but no one could find anything wrong with her.

After praying for Chanel, Dad and the assistant pastor went back to pray for my mom again. As they finished praying for her, she opened her eyes. She immediately began asking questions about what had happened, but she could not remember what happened or how the accident occurred. The doctors came in to check my mom again and found that she had no serious injuries or broken bones. She had a few minor scratches, but aside from that, she was completely healed. After a final check, the doctors allowed Mom to go home, but they decided to keep Chanel overnight for observation. They were utterly baffled by the way that God had healed her instantly; they wanted to make sure she really was healed.

Before going home, my parents were notified of my critical condition. My injuries were severe and had also caused internal bleeding. The surgeons were going to begin a 10.5-hour microscopic surgery to try to reconstruct the bones and save my arm, hand, and fingers. However, they were going to have to give me high doses of morphine and anesthesia. They warned my parents that the doses were too high for a forty-five-day-old baby. They said that if I did not die from my injuries, I could die from the high doses of morphine and sedatives. My parents were asked to sign waivers releasing the hospital from liability in the event of my death. They went home and I went into surgery.

The next day, my parents returned to the hospital to check on my sister and me. My sister was completely fine. She had no injuries and was released that afternoon. I was moved to the intensive care unit and was recovering from surgery. I was heavily sedated and was not awake or coherent. The doctors explained again that the situation was still critical. During the surgery, both of my lungs had collapsed. They were able to get me to start breathing again, but I made it through the surgery with the use of only one lung. They had to put metal wires inside my arm, hand, and fingers to try to reconstruct the arm and hold it in place. During my recovery, I was strapped to a bed, and my dad said he remembers my mom crying because she could not hold me. Despite all of these circumstances, the church continued to pray for my recovery and healing.

After a few days, the doctors came back to my parents to talk about my progress. They were worried because part of my hand and all of my fingers were still completely black, which meant that the blood was not circulating properly. They warned that gangrene could set in and cause an infection that would spread throughout the arm and into the rest of my body. They wanted to amputate my arm up to the humerus (upper arm). My parents rejected the request to amputate, and they continued to pray, as did the rest of our church members. The prayers worked, because a few days later, part of my arm and three of my fingers turned pink (a sign of healthy blood flow and new skin), and the doctors were pleased with my progress.

After a few days had passed, there was no further improvement. My left index and ring fingers were completely dead and shriveled up. The bone in my middle finger had also rotted because of the dead fingers. The doctors said they could not wait any longer to amputate the remaining two fingers and remove the rotted bone from my middle finger. They began preparing for another major surgery. My parents were asked to sign waivers again, because the amount of anesthesia and sedatives needed for such a major surgery could have killed me. The day of the surgery arrived, and my parents were in the hospital nursery, visiting me before my surgery. As they visited, my dad felt the angel of death enter the hospital. He told my mom that they needed to head to the church immediately.

When they got to the church, Dad knocked on the pastor's door and asked to speak with him. He ushered them into the office, and my dad told the pastor that while they were visiting me, he had felt the angel of death enter the hospital. His pastor told him he would have to do the hardest thing that he had ever done in his life. He told Dad to go to the altar with my mom, and together they would have to surrender their baby to God.

He said, "You need to give your baby to God. If He wants to take her today, you need to give her to Him." They went to the altar and wept and prayed together. They completely surrendered me to God that day, and then they got up from the altar and drove back to the hospital. On the drive back, the Holy Ghost filled the car, and my Mom began to travail in the Spirit. She prayed for me all the way to the hospital. When they walked through the doors of the hospital, a baby was being wheeled out of the surgery ward on a gurney, covered with a sheet.

Mom grabbed Dad's arm and shouted, "Gerry!"

He grabbed her hand and said, "Don't worry, let me go check on her." He went to the nurse's desk and asked about me. The nurse told him to hold on a minute so she could get an update for him. She came back and informed him that I was still in surgery but that I was doing fine. They were relieved, and after the surgery was complete, they were allowed to visit my room.

When my parents entered my room, I was awake and drinking water. They were informed that the surgery had gone well. However, on the operating table, one of my lungs had collapsed again. Despite that, the surgeons had successfully amputated two fingers on my left hand and removed the rotted bone from the left middle finger. I had over 200 stitches that stretched from my upper arm (where my elbow had been pushed up) down to my hand and fingers. Throughout my recovery, my mom was allowed to stay with me and, eventually, I was put in my own hospital room. After a few weeks, the metal wires holding my arm and fingers into place were removed and I was allowed to go home (I was just over three months). My mom learned to care for my arm and hand. She had to change my bandages and clean my wounds so that I would heal properly. When my wounds completely healed, and the stitches were removed, I started physical therapy. I learned to strengthen my arm and hand and use them properly, and after three years, I completed my therapy. Even though my physical wounds had healed, I still had a long road of healing and recovery ahead of me.

Growing Up
Even though I had no recollection of the accident, I did not realize that the trauma had left a lasting effect on me. I

was a sensitive, shy, emotional child. I cried all the time and was afraid of everything. I was extremely close to my mother and did not like to be away from her. Even though I was a bundle of nerves and tears, my parents raised me in a beautiful, supportive way. They treated me like a normal kid. They were attentive and sensitive to my needs, but they never allowed me to wallow in self-pity.

Two specific instances stand out to me that demonstrate just how supportive they were. When I was four, my parents were teaching me how to tie my shoes. I would get so frustrated that I would cry, and they would end up tying my shoes for me. One day, we were getting ready to go out, and I was putting on my tennis shoes. I asked my dad to tie my shoes, and he said, "No." I remember looking up at him in shock and telling him that he needed to tie my shoes because I couldn't tie them because of my hand. He told me that I could indeed tie them. I started to cry and told him I couldn't do it. He sat down with me on the floor and showed me how to tie my shoes over and over again until I could tie them all by myself. When I finally tied them on my own, I felt so triumphant.

I beamed up at him, and he told me, "Don't ever say that you can't do something, because you can."

Another time, when I was ten, I was trying to comb my own hair (before then my mom or sister combed my hair for me). I had tried several times, but I couldn't get it right. I got so frustrated that I threw the brush down and started crying. My mom came into the bathroom and asked what was wrong. With tears running down my face, I told her that I couldn't comb my hair because of my hand. She hugged me and started to cry. We cried together for a time, and then she set me away from her and tilted my chin up so I could look at her.

She said, "Don't you ever say that you can't do something. You can do whatever you want to do. Don't ever use your hand as an excuse. You CAN do it, and you WILL do it." And eventually, I did.

My parents never treated me like an invalid or a handicap. They always encouraged me to try new things, and I was treated just like my other two sisters. I wasn't allowed to make excuses for why I couldn't do something, and I wasn't allowed to say, "I can't." I learned to use my left hand to its fullest capacity, but I was always insecure and shy. I leaned heavily on my family for emotional support. Being raised in such a positive, sheltered environment did not prepare me for life outside of my home and family.

Not everyone saw me the way my family did, nor did they treat me the same. They saw my arm and hand and immediately put limits on me. For instance, when I was in the second grade at our church's Christian school, I was at recess playing outside. I was in line to play four square, and when it was my turn, the kids wouldn't let me play because they said I wouldn't be able to catch the ball because of my hand. I was embarrassed and ashamed. This was one of the first times I realized that I was different from everyone else. Similar situations happened several times throughout my childhood, and I didn't realize how they shaped my own views of myself until I was older. Even though I received love and support at home, I couldn't understand why other people didn't treat me like my parents did.

When I was ten years old, I decided that I wanted to learn to play the piano. I talked to my parents about it, and of course, they were fully supportive, and we found someone to give me piano lessons. I was so excited, and I couldn't wait to start. I remember talking with my mom on the ride over to the piano teacher's house; I was ecstatic. When I got there, seven or eight other students were already there, sitting at piano keyboards. My teacher pulled me aside and proceeded to tell me that I would only be able to progress to a certain point because of my hand and lack of fingers. She said there were songs I wouldn't be able to play and that I might have some trouble playing. I immediately felt discouraged, and ashamed of myself. I also felt foolish for even attempting such a feat. I decided that I would not continue lessons. However, my parents did not let me quit. They told me that a commitment was important and that I should not let go of my dream because of what other people thought or said.

As I continued to learn piano and grow as a musician, I found that I had a talent for singing as well. (Only God could give a voice to sing to someone who had their lungs collapse twice.) I would practice for hours and get lost in the music. I sang all the time and I loved worship songs. My passion for music and worship only grew with time. By the age of thirteen, I was singing and playing at church, but I always compared myself to other musicians. I felt that my playing was not good enough. I feared that I would never be as good as the others because I was missing fingers on my left hand. However, I carried myself like a normal person (because of my upbringing), and people would hardly notice my hand, if at all. However, in my heart, I was never pleased with my talent and skill. I continued to play and sing and God began to use me, but deep down, I was unhappy and ashamed of my hand.

The Healing

As I grew older, I began to question why God would let such a life-changing accident happen to me. I couldn't understand how God could love me and let something like that happen to me. I didn't want to be different. I wanted my fingers back and I wanted my ugly scars to go away. I set my hopes on being healed. When preachers would come to our church and preach about miracles and healing, I was always one of the first ones to the altar. I would cry and plead with God to heal my left hand and let new fingers grow.

I would try to bargain with God, and tell Him, "If you give me new fingers, I will do anything for You." I told God, "I can tell people about what a miracle you did in my life because you gave me new fingers." But every time I prayed for a miracle, it never came. The preachers would shout, "Your miracle is here; receive it!" and I would squeeze my eyes shut and beg and plead with God for a miracle. Then, I would slowly open my eyes and look down at my hand. But it looked the same: ugly, mangled, and scarred.

I began to grow angry with God and question why He wouldn't heal me. I decided it was because He didn't love me enough. I thought He was ashamed of me and I didn't understand why He would let me live this way. Insecurity spread into other areas of my life, and eventually, I became a sensitive, needy person with a fragile, broken heart. I didn't realize that my healing needed to come from within.

Throughout my teenage years, I continued to sing and play at church, but I wrestled constantly with my own insecurities about my left hand. I was ashamed of myself, and I wanted to be like everyone else. Although God continued to use me, I could not fully love or accept myself. But God continued to be patient with me, and as I grew older, He began to mend my heart. I can remember specific times when a ministry prayed for me and deep healing would come. Once, a minister prayed for me and he said, "Let God heal the areas of your heart that are too painful to touch. He loves you and He wants to heal your heart, He doesn't want you to hurt inside." That night, God touched my heart so deeply that I couldn't breathe because the emotional pain was so great. Another time, we had a minister with a prophetic ministry come to our church. After the altar call, he walked the aisles, and he asked me to stand up and raise my hands. When I looked into his eyes, I felt like he could see to the very core of my soul. He said that the first time he heard me sing and play, he couldn't reconcile the beautiful sound with what was in my heart. He began to tell me about how I questioned why God would let this happen to me. He said God gave him a vision of me sitting in my room crying and being angry with God about my hand. He prayed for me, and I felt God's love and healing flow over me. From that day on, I have never looked at myself the same way. I let go of the "why" and stopped trying to understand it all. I surrendered to God completely, and He has continued to heal me and use my talents for His glory. I have embraced my calling completely and God has continued to open doors for me to minister in music, teach vocal and piano lessons, and give music workshops. I have dedicated my life to answering his call and bringing him glory.

Even now, God continues to heal my heart and show me His love. The other day, I was talking with my dad, and he started to tell me about how God marked people in the Bible. He told me, "When I look at you, I don't see scars and missing fingers, I see the mark of God." He said, "You are marked by God, and he uses you for his glory." I had never thought of my scars and hand in that way. How humbling to be marked by God and to be used in a way that brings him glory! I began to think about how God had taken the things that I hated about myself, and now He uses them for His glory. He uses my lungs (the ones that collapsed twice) and voice to sing His praise. He uses my disfigured hand to play music that brings Him glory.

Now when I look at my scars and hand, I see grace and mercy. I see a love that transcends understanding. Only God could take a tragedy and turn it into a victory. When I look in the mirror, I see a living, breathing, walking miracle. Whenever I feel myself start to wallow in self-pity and shame, I hold firm to I Corinthians 12:9, which says, "And he said unto me, My grace is sufficient for thee: for my strength is made perfect in weakness. Most gladly, therefore, will I rather glory in my infirmities, that the power of Christ may rest upon me."

In His eyes, I am fearfully and wonderfully made. I am whole. I am beautiful. I am complete. I lack nothing because His grace is sufficient for me. He uses my weaknesses for his glory. He doesn't see me the way others see me. He sees me through eyes of love. He has a plan for my life and He sees who I can be. He has been right beside me even before I was fully aware of His presence. And because of Him, I am alive today, a living testament to His love, His mercy, and His grace...a young woman marked by God, for His glory.

> Contac information for speaking engagements:
> Marin.samantha@gmail.com

Isabel Clavesilla

Carlos Ceniceros

Richard Ceniceros

Mark Thomas (Stucker)

Three Generations

CHAPTER 4

Isabel Clavesilla

I really don't know where to begin. There are so many things of which I could speak. When I was asked to be a part of this, I remembered a friend years ago had mentioned, "Isabel, you need to write your story down. Others need to hear what God has done for you and through you." So, when George Pantages asked me, I had no hesitation. We have nothing greater to give back to the Lord than our worship and the word of our testimony. The Word, the gifts, and the anointing all belong to Him. Since the Garden of Eden, God has longed for relationship with His creation. This is about Jesus Christ. Truthfully, all I know is the Lord.

My father, Carlos Ceniceros Sr., before he came to the Lord, was a slave to heroin for over twenty years. He was a dictator. He taught us, his children, to trust no man and also what happened in our house stayed in our house. My father did teach us to stick together, to be bold, and to be fearless. If we were going to fear anything, it was going to be him. But I can honestly say that there was a method to his madness, and I thank God for that. My mother was raised in the church, but never got baptized until later in life. I learned denial of self at an early age, and not by choice. I learned to fear no man. But somehow, I learned to fear the Lord and that the fear of the Lord is the beginning of wisdom.

One of my early memories was when I was five years old. I was at a family party and I began to feel very sick. I started vomiting and couldn't stop. I had such a high fever they took me to the emergency room at the old County General Hospital in Los Angeles. They told my parents I had contracted polio. Back then, there was no vaccine against polio, and it was known as a crippling disease, causing paralysis with no cure. I was so little, and I didn't understand why I had to stay at the hospital and not go home with my family. I was there for at least six months and had braces on my legs to walk. I remember my family would come on the weekends to see me, but they had to wear masks. I thank God I had a praying grandmother, Sis. Rosas, and I truly believe her prayers brought me through. I remember when I was able to come home, my brothers had to carry me from the car and wherever I needed to go. I remember every day my mother would have to exercise my legs. She would lay me on the kitchen table and move my legs. I was too young to understand what was happening. I didn't mind any of it because I was just so

Isabel Clavesilla

happy to be home with my family. Many children who got polio didn't make it. Today, the only effects I have from having polio are that one hip is slightly higher than the other and one leg is a little shorter than the other. I thank God for my grandmother's prayers.

I came to the Lord as a young woman. My brother, Carlos, was the first one in my family to be baptized and receive the Holy Ghost, then me, followed by my brothers and parents. I always thought that when you gave your heart to the Lord, that everything would go right. I would like to say I had a honeymoon experience when I came to the Lord, but that is not my story. I was baptized in water as a young woman went directly up to Camp Seely for youth camp. It was there that I received the Holy Ghost, speaking in tongues for the first time. I remember coming down from the mountain, being so excited. I couldn't wait to share my experience with everyone, only to learn that the father of my three-month-old daughter had been killed in a freak accident. During that time, I was feeling very confused, because up to that point, everything seemed like it was coming together for me. I couldn't understand why the Lord removed the man I loved, leaving me and my daughter without him. I didn't think my heart would ever heal. This was the beginning of my "being born again" experience, and it was nothing like I had imagined. I was devastated.

It took about three years for me to be able to let someone else into my heart. Tom was a kind and loving man. I felt a love from him that I had never really experienced before. He was the love of my life. But as the years went by, I realized that he had weaknesses from his own childhood pain that led him to drug abuse. I believe Tom took drugs to sedate or anesthetize himself, in an attempt to numb his mental and emotional pain. He didn't have the tools or the experience to know how to be a husband, father and a provider for his family. I believe he realized he wasn't able to be those things, and I think that gave him permission to walk out on me and our children. I was heartbroken again. I was raised and taught "once married, always married." Maybe it was just because my husband took my heart, but I never considered remarrying after Tom -- it wasn't even a thought. My loyalties were to my children. I had a mother who was loyal, so I learned that from her. At this point, I was beyond devastated. I was shattered.

During this time of brokenness, I left California and I joined my brother, Carlos Ceniceros, Jr., and his family, who were missionaries in New York. After a few months of being there, I was picking up children for Sunday school and my three-year-old son fell out of the car and died instantly. When my husband left me, I was so hurt, and so lost. But when I lost my son, it was different. I birthed that child. I was connected to him and he was a part of me. I don't think there is any greater loss or depth of despair that anyone can experience than the loss of a child. The one thing that kept me during this time was that I remembered I had always prayed to the Lord, "If my children are not going to serve You, Lord, take them." I remember being on the plane flying back to Los Angeles to bury my son, knowing while I was in the plane, my son's body was in the cargo section of the same plane with the luggage. My heart was broken into pieces. Pastor Willie Mendoza preached my son's funeral. He used the text from Jeremiah 29:11, *"For I know the plans I have for you," declares the Lord, "plans to prosper you and not to harm you, plans to give you hope and a future."* At the time, I was so broken, I couldn't even receive the scripture. I will say this, the loss of my son taught me the value of humanity. For me, the most important thing this side of heaven is people. I found out that we're here today and gone tomorrow. This experience transformed my character and life forever, and I'm thankful.

Shortly after that, there was the loss of my brother, Richard, who was ten months younger than me. My memories of Richard growing up are that he was a very sick boy. He suffered from asthma at a time when there really weren't the medications that we have now. I remember my mother sitting him on her lap, fanning him constantly. It seemed to help him with his breathing. My mother would have to take him to the hospital all the time for breathing treatments. By that time, my mother had given birth to my youngest brother, Ernie. Because my mother was always having to care for Richard, I had to take care of Ernie. I became like a second mother to him.

Richard did get better as he got to his teenage years. He was only twenty-five years old when, after a watchnight service in the Compton Church on New Year's Eve, he left the house to go to the grocery store to buy some beverages for the family, and never came back. We received a phone call at 4:00 the next morning that he had been hit by a stray bullet and found dead in an alley. Once again, I was devastated.

All of these things happened while I was still in my twenties. Though we weren't raised in the church, when we came to the Lord, we all got busy in kingdom work. My brothers were called to different places -- Texas, New York, and I got involved in local ministry [Southern California]. During those early years of brokenness, even though I was surrounded by people and was involved in church, I was very much alone, separated by grief and heartbreak. But through my brokenness, I had no choice but to lean on the Lord Jesus Christ. I never knew at the time that I was, in fact, building a relationship with the Lord that would eventually make me who I am today.

About ten years after my son died, my oldest grandson was about the same age as my son was when he died. My grandson used to say things that my son used to say, and when he died, I began grieving my son all over again. I thought I was losing my mind. At that time, I was involved in a serious car accident. As the car was spinning, I remember thinking, "I have felt this way before -- but when was I here?" All of a sudden, the Lord brought it to my mind. I felt this way when my son fell out of the car door. I thought I had grieved the loss of my son when I lost him, but this went so much deeper -- it's hard to find the right words. I told my daughters that I needed to separate myself, and I closed myself in my room to pray. I called friends who I knew would pray for me. I don't think I did a lot of praying, but I did do a lot of crying. The Lord showed me that if He had allowed me to grieve to this depth when my son died, I wouldn't have made it mentally and emotionally. The Lord showed me it was time to grieve deeply enough so that He could heal me and make me whole.

Grieving losses is so important. Pain and despair can take you to a place where you must choose to let go. There have been many people I have met over the years, and I have heard it said, "If you had known them before their loss they were completely different." In my experience, that "completely different" is a choice. I realized that people who end up in mental institutions or in a state of deep depression, somewhere they gave up. In that letting go, there is a sense of freedom -- they don't have responsibilities, there are no expectations, and they don't have to be accountable for their lives. That is their choice, not the Lord's.

Now the message is all about inner healing. I didn't realize at the time that God was using my brokenness to walk me through the journey of self. Growing up, I never learned to get outside help. Had I known about mentors or having a one-on-one with somebody, I might have gone on this journey a lot sooner. But maybe it was the will of God the whole time for me to be totally schooled by Him. I don't remember ever reading a self-help book. I don't ever remember leaning on my own understanding, because I had none. Even though I was alone, I don't ever remember feeling lonely. I honestly cannot accept it when people speak about loneliness. For me, loneliness is godlessness. If you have the Holy Ghost, you are never really alone. He has made His dwelling place within us. If you are lonely, you are living beneath your privileges and have not tapped into what is available in the Holy Ghost.

I remember early in my walk with God being enamored with my sisters in the Lord. Enamored with their teachings and thinking I would never be able to do that. I couldn't even memorize a verse. My pastor told me that I needed to connect with my sisters in the Lord because I had a lot to say. Slowly but surely, I began to interact more with them. One day, I realized one of them was being very unkind. I looked at her, and the Lord spoke to me in an intimate way and said, "Isabel, they know the Word of God, but you know the God of the Word." Those words resonated within me. I thought about it, and I realized it is not about knowledge or about teaching, it is about relationship. The Lord was letting me know, "You know

Me, and you walk with Me." I remember that day, and because of His words the tears flowed like an uncontrollable river. Here I had put myself beneath everyone else, when nothing could be further from the truth. All my friends were getting married, buying houses and having kids, and everything in their lives seemed to be going well. There were times I thought, "Will it ever happen for me?" Anyone who knows me or who has been around me knows it has never been about money, never been about a career, never been about knowledge. It has always been about people. I never really had the opportunity to dream or plan. Because of my brokenness and the stripping away of everything that was dear to me, the world lost its glitter for me at a young age.

I have had many other losses in my life, including the deaths of my father, and my oldest brother, Carlos. About five years ago, I almost lost my youngest brother, Ernie, when he jumped out of a second-floor window while hallucinating on drugs. I remember the ambulance came and took him. We lost him two times on the way to the hospital, and once again on the operating room table. Ernie was in a coma for nine days. I remember the doctors didn't give us much hope for his survival, and we were told to prepare for the worst. I remember the whole time knowing beyond a shadow of a doubt in my spirit that no demon was going to take my brother out like that. I was adamant that Ernie was going to live. I remember my brother, Rudy telling me, "Isabel, we need to prepare Mom." I told him, "No. You prepare Mom. Ernie is going to make it." When the doctors came and told me that they wanted to amputate his arm due to the injuries he sustained in his fall, they explained that Ernie's arm had lost circulation and they needed to take it. I said, "No. my brother is not going to wake up missing his arm." No one believed Ernie was going to make it. I remember everyone was showing their emotions at the hospital and I wouldn't shed a tear. Only when Ernie came out of the coma and was transferred to Rancho Los Amigos hospital for rehabilitation was I able to break. I believe to this day that the Lord kept him because He is not done with him. Ernie is the brother who always felt that he had no ministry, and that was not the truth. His ministry is yet to be seen.

One of the things I am most thankful for in my life is that I did have a praying grandmother. I remember in her last years, I would take care of her on the weekends. I would say to her, "Grandma, are you ready to go home?" She would name all her children and grandchildren one by one who she still needed to pray for. She wouldn't name me. I remember saying to her one day, "Grandma, you never say my name." She answered, "Oh Mija, you have everything." "I do, Grandma? What do I have?" "Well, you have the Lord. You have a good report. And considering everything you have gone through, He has given you a sound mind." It never dawned on me what she was really saying, until I saw her in her coffin. I walked up to her and as I looked at her, the Lord brought her words back to me. The Lord spoke to me again in an intimate way, "I can be found. A good report can be obtained. But a sound mind, only I can give."

I know that God and God alone rescued me and kept my mind. I do believe that the voice of God does speak to us, whether in our subconscious or an audible voice. Any one of us who has the Holy Ghost, the Lord lives within us and He desires to speak and is speaking. He is God of everything, or He is God of nothing.

Today, there is a home for women in Whittier, CA. It is called Dwelling in the Secret Place. It is named after Psalm 91:1, *"He who dwelleth in the secret place of the Most High shall abide under the shadow of the Almighty."* When my father passed away, I heard from the platform during his funeral, "The mantle of the father has been passed to his daughter, Isabel." My father got to see the outside of the house, but died before having the chance to see the birthing of this ministry. I never recognized or connected the reality that opening a faith-based home for women was my desire. I believe the Lord honored my father's burden, and his calling lives on.

Today, I am considered a woman of prayer. The bigger truth is that this was never by choice. I had no choice. My journey in living for God meant experiencing tragedy after tragedy. I am familiar with death and have had many losses and disappointments. I suffered mistreatment. For years, I remember my prayers were, "Lord, no matter what happens, please don't let go of me." I know now that I was not stripped, abused, and broken without purpose. I really don't recognize that girl back there, but I never forget her, because without her, I wouldn't be the woman of God that I am today. I say that with boldness, because the world didn't give it and the world can't take it away. As I look back over my journey in life, I can truthfully say the Lord has kept me. All I had was the Lord in my brokenness, and truthfully that is all we really need. He has become my everything. I have not veered from that. It is in dying to self that true ministry is birthed. Let us never forget that wherever we go, we have a platform to speak -- whether it be to family, friends, co-workers or people we meet on the street. Whatever we have been through is not just for our experience, but to be able to pass it on to someone else. Because the power of God is in the word of our testimony.

Contac information for speaking engagements:
Isabel@dwellinginthesecretplace.org

Unique Arreaga

With Evangelist Mingo Garcia

At Youth Camp

CHAPTER 5

Unique Arreaga

Hi, my name is Unique Arreaga, and I'm seventeen years old. I attend Apostolic Faith Center Church in Whittier, California, under Pastors Isaac and Angela Hernandez. My father, Gilbert Arreaga currently serves as the assistant pastor, aided by my mom, Josie Arreaga. I want to give a little background before I share what the Lord has done in my life. I was born and raised Apostolic; my parents are very involved in the church, so we spend a lot of time serving in the house of God. I sing on the praise team and I am also the director of the media department. I have had the privilege, ever since I can remember, to attend private Christian schools (K-8). When I graduated from eighth grade, my parents decided that I would attend public school for the first time. My brother was already a sophomore at Temple City High School in California, but I was not really excited about going to public school because all of my friends were attending another private Christian school in another city. This was a difficult time for me because it was a very large school, and basically my brother and I were the only Apostolics there amongst 4,500 students. I have always been very active in sports, especially soccer, and my parents kept me very busy with church and sports. But I always had more friends at school than at church, mainly because my church is very small, and I really never had the desire to go and visit other churches to make new friends. I adapted well at Temple City High, made a lot of new friends, and later realized they were not the best influences for my walk with God. At this time I was fifteen years old, a sophomore, and it was my second year playing at a high level of soccer.

    I remember it was around March, the end of the soccer season, when God started to take me on a life-changing journey. I was warming up one day at practice, doing my normal routine stretching, and I felt a sharp pain. I didn't think much of it at the time. I just thought maybe I was a little sore from my game or practice earlier in the week, so I left it alone. A few months later, in May, I felt the pain again when I was getting out of bed. I was very curious and started to wonder what could be making my back hurt when I was moving a certain way. I hadn't done anything out of the ordinary, so I started to massage the area that was hurting. At that time, I felt a lump the size of a small ball, and it was located on my back where the sharp pain was. I began to think that maybe I had torn a muscle or had a bruise.

I really didn't want to tell my parents because I wasn't on the best terms with them. I had been put on restriction because I was not making the best choices at school. But I decided to tell them anyway. Normally, my mom is the one always the most concerned, but she thought I hit myself during soccer and did not think twice about it. On the other hand, my dad is the tough love type, he would most likely say, "Suck it up, you're fine," but this time it was totally different because he insisted that she make an appointment immediately. So, my mom made my appointment. I thought I was going to see my doctor within a month, because the doctor was always so busy. But this time was different, they scheduled me in within two days. Once the doctor saw me and felt the lump, he scheduled an x-ray on the same day, and surprisingly the x-ray didn't show anything. But my doctor wasn't satisfied with the results because he knew what he felt and there had to be something wrong. The next step the doctor wanted to take was a biopsy, meaning they basically wanted to take some samples of my tissue. When you go to these types of centers, they don't tell you immediately what the results are. I remember the doctor telling my mom they would send the results to my primary doctor, but really, he reassured my mom that normally these results just scratched the surface. We left there just wondering what this could be.

At this time, I was struggling with my walk with God. I knew I wasn't living the way I should, and most certainly not the way my parents taught me.

I always had this image that preachers' kids had to be perfect, and I knew that I wasn't that! I was so far away from God, born and raised under the pews, and on my way to Hell if the Lord came that night. I was very bitter and trying to do my own thing. I was more focused on school life than my spiritual walk with God. My parents talked to my pastor and asked if their daughter, Brooke could talk to me to see if she could help me in any way. I remember that morning she came, and she took me out for breakfast to talk. She began to share her story with me as a pastor's daughter. She was able to relate to me when she was younger because she had gone through the same thing I was going through. I felt like she was sharing hope with me. I didn't want to sin against God or have that guilt that would weigh on my heart. The advice I got was that it was time for me to get closer to God, and I needed to have my own relationship with the Lord, one that would be up close and personal. I had to make sure that I really prayed and fasted and not just pretend or fall asleep during morning prayer at my house. One rule that my dad established was prayer in the morning. No one left the house without praying. Hearing the Word being preached would no longer be enough, I actually had to read the Word on my own as well.

At this point, the week of June 23, 2017, my doctor called my parents with the results of my biopsy and told them the lump on my lower back was cancerous. My parents were speechless and were at a loss for words, waiting for the appropriate time to tell me. The doctor immediately put in an emergency request for me to see a specialist at Children's Hospital of Orange County. They specialize in the treating of cancer at any age. I remember my mom getting off work early, which was out of the ordinary. My parents called me into their room and told me that my doctor had called them back about my results. It was CANCER! It wasn't what I thought it would be, because when you think of cancer you immediately think of death. My first response was to think that they were joking, so I started to laugh. I thought they were trying to scare me into serving God, but they both cried and said no. I couldn't understand why I would have cancer, and my mind went racing out of control. My mom and dad told me that now wasn't the time to be angry with God, but it was time to get closer to God. After that, we just went on with the day. The word cancer just continued to echo through my mind. I had many nights that I would just cry myself to sleep, and other nights that I simply didn't sleep. It was a scary, dark moment in my life, and as silly as it might sound, I was scared to sleep at night. I'd have nightmares, but it was just the devil trying to discourage me and trying to make me feel hopeless during this time. But I still kept a smile on my face, and I listened to my parents and tried to stay positive, because there was no room for negativity. I always remembered what my primary doctor told my mom. He said, "Unique is not going to die of cancer. She is too stubborn." He knew me well! He had been my doctor since my birth.

 Then Sunday came and my family went to church as usual. My dad announced to my church that I had cancer. He briefly said that this was simply a test that our family was going to endure. He also said that this was going to be a time for us to seek God and to trust in Him through this time. I sat there feeling empty, sad, and confused at the same time. Normally we didn't have special speakers, but that Sunday was different. Rev. Jonathan Cruz from Boise, Idaho, walked through the doors shortly after my dad had announced my situation, so he didn't hear anything that my dad had said. The preacher walked up on the platform and started his message by saying, "I don't know what had happened before I came in. I remember he was looking straight at me. He then pointed at me and prophesied that

God was going to put me through a test, not to harm me but to see if I believed in Him for myself, not for what my parents or what your pastor or youth leader told me. I was so shocked with what he said, because not only did he tell me the exact thing my parents, pastor, and youth leaders were all trying to convince me of, but at that moment I knew it wasn't by coincidence that all these people were telling me the same thing. I knew it was all God, because during this time it was so hard for me, knowing that I had cancer.

Youth camp was a week away. My parents had paid for me to attend one month before my diagnosis. I didn't really want to go before all this happened, and when my parents brought it up again, I was thinking, "Like really, I just got diagnosed with cancer. Like this is the last thing on my mind," but at the last minute I decided to go. I knew that this would help me get closer to God, just to get out the house, and fellowship with other Apostolic youth. It was July 2, the first day of youth camp, my parents drove me and my brother to camp.

I wasn't excited to go to camp. Honestly, I was pretty nervous to go because I didn't really have any friends from church. All my other friends were from school. The fact of sharing a cabin with girls I didn't know for a week made me feel a little uncomfortable. Evangelist Mingo Garcia was the special speaker for youth camp. I had never heard him preach until camp, but people were telling me that he was an amazing preacher.

I have to agree: he is truly an anointed man of God. I could relate to his teachings so much. It wasn't even altar call and I was already bawling my eyes out. God really spoke to me those few nights at camp.

I decided to befriend the girls I was sharing a cabin with. I never mentioned to anyone I had cancer, I wanted to just feel normal. One night, we were all telling each other about ourselves, and I told them I had to leave camp early. When they asked why, I told them that I had cancer and I was leaving because I was going to see a specialist. My cabin room got real quiet. They were all shocked and asked if I was joking, and I told them that I wasn't. I explained to the girls that I had a lump on my lower back that was cancerous. They had no clue that I had cancer because I acted normal, I always looked happy. My body language didn't show I was scared. My dad had told my family that we were going to confuse the enemy and act like everything was good.

For the first time I was happy, I was making new friends and they were from church! Everyone was sad that I had to leave camp early. I had been to camps before, but this time was different. I had the best time! At this point, the girls from my cabin, my brother, and my youth leader were the only ones who knew about my situation. Wednesday night, July 5 was an altar call, and Mingo was praying for my older brother, Joseph. After he finished praying for him, Joseph asked Mingo if he'd go and pray for me because I had been diagnosed with cancer. The preacher asked my brother to go and look for my youth leader, David Hernandez. Both Mingo and David called me over to the altar. That night was amazing, Mingo asked if I would be okay with coming on the stage. He asked my name and age. He also announced to all the campers that I had been diagnosed with cancer. I didn't know what type of cancer I had, all I knew was that I was going to see the oncologist, therefore I had to leave camp early the next morning. At that moment, the question was asked to all the campers if they wanted to see God do a healing from cancer. They asked everyone to come to the altar and join in a special prayer. Every camper came to the altar and he asked for all the brave girls to come up on the stage. All the sisters gave me a hug and said words of encouragement to me. The service was live on social media and I cried the whole service, leaving everything in God's hands. I believe that night I received my healing.

Thursday morning came, and it was time for me to leave. I wasn't happy that I had to leave camp, but I was happy to make some new friends. Denise, Giselle, Ariana and Sammie, the youth of Bethel Temple in Santa Ana, became a great support system for me.

When I left camp, I had joy and peace. I wasn't scared of what the doctors were going to say because I had put all my trust in God, and I knew He wouldn't put me through something I couldn't handle. Jeremiah 29:11 comes to mind: "I know the plans I have for you, says to Lord, plans to prosper you and not to harm you, plans to give you hope and a future." Both of my parents took me to my appointment and told me that I had primary neoplasm, a cancerous tumor that young adolescents can develop, and it was in the early stages. If I had waited longer, it could have been worse.

I was scheduled immediately for an MRI and a CAT scan. Surgery was scheduled within two weeks to remove the tumor, which was two weeks before my sixteenth birthday. I was going to celebrate my birthday in Cancun, Mexico, but my family had to cancel the trip. So, before surgery my parents decided to go up to Monterey. We spent time around each other near the beach. Well, being from an Apostolic home, when you are on vacation, somehow you end up going to church on vacation. So we ended up taking a detour on our way home and went up to Stockton to visit Bishop Joe Mendoza's church. While we were there, they made a special prayer for me and it just so happened that Pastor Dan Duarte from Youngstown, AZ, was there. He is great friends with my parents, so when the altar call came, he came up and prayed for my parents and it felt so personal. He gave us all a word from the Lord, and all I remember was that he said, "Don't worry about anything, it's been sealed, and you are healed." We left encouraged and I went back home to prepare for surgery.

I was able to visit one more church before my surgery. I attended Bethel Temple in Santa Ana, where all my new friends were from. Pastor Ruben Villegas called me up and asked if I would introduce myself to the congregation. I was blessed being there, as he mentioned the youth came back on fire for God. He also thanked me for having an impact on the youth. He was so thankful, because out of the seven young people from his church who went to camp, five of them got baptized in the name of Jesus when they returned from camp. I was happy for them that they all made that decision to fully dedicate their lives to God. This was all because they had met me and didn't want to play with the things of God. The church was also praying for me, believing that God would heal. I thought I was the only one blessed by meeting their youth. They were all so supportive and kind to me. I'm thankful for every one of them because they befriended me when I needed some godly friends at the most difficult time of my life. It was a special day for me because it was August 6, my sixteenth birthday, and I was able to be in the house of the Lord and celebrate it with my friends. The service ended up with prayer, and after service a sister from the church came and prayed with me. She told me that she was a cancer survivor and she was going to pray for me. I felt so much love and support.

Tuesday, August 8, two days after my sixteenth birthday, was my surgery date. We had to be at the hospital early at 6:30am. It was a cold day, walking into the hospital. Shortly they called us into an office room to tell us about the procedure that was going to take place. Surgery was estimated to be three hours long. The process began when I got my gown on, the IVs were placed at that moment, and my dad said a prayer for me. I was wheeled into the area where anesthesiologist talked to me. He started to give me the anesthesia. I remember being asked a couple questions and fell asleep. I was awakened by the nurse, and could hear children crying. The nurse was telling me I woke up so peaceful, compared to the other patients, who were violent and hostile. I was very calm, mostly tired, but my nurse said that they would bring over my parents and my brother in a few minutes. It literally felt like I just closed my eyes and it was all over.

My parents went out to breakfast because they were told it would be three hours until they could see me. They ended up coming back early and noticed that the doctor was in the waiting room, looking for them. My parents described the look on the doctor's face was as if she had seen a ghost, utterly lost for words. My parents began to think something she ate was wrong.

They asked, "Is Unique okay?"

She replied, "Yes, but I want to explain something to you." She explained that the tumor was so deep into my tissue, she couldn't understand how we were all able to feel it. She said that she had to dig and dig to get it out, and when she finally was able to reach it, it was simply just sitting on top of my muscle in my lower back / lumbar area. But that's not what she wanted to focus on. She couldn't explain it, but she said that the cancer had dried up from the inside out, and all the cells deteriorated and died, and did not have time to spread into any of my organs. She also said she went back to look at the MRI and that the pathology report stated that the cancer dried up from the inside out. My parents were left there in the waiting area, looking at each other and thinking, "What just happened?" They thanked the doctor for all the work that she had done for me. When they were left alone, they knew that God healed me. My parents finally came to see me. I told them I felt fine.

All I was able to eat was a strawberry popsicle in the recovery room. Shortly after that, I was wheeled into my room that I would be staying in for the next few days. I had been fasting since the night before and all I could think of was food, so my parents went out to get me something to eat. I could feel the tightness on my back, but no pain. I was highly medicated. My parents shared the news about my surgery and explained what the doctor told them, and I knew God had healed me! God would get the glory and I was going to share this with everyone. I was happy that I was healed, and shocked at the same time.

I had about twenty visitors come and see me! I was fine with visitors, so all my friends I made at camp came to visit me. I was overwhelmed with joy that they came. My church family came to visit also. Everyone said I looked great. I felt totally fine, just really tired and drained. I was thankful for all the flowers and balloons. Revival started at my church. The people of God were encouraged through what the

Lord had done in my life. I ended up having to share my room with a young toddler, so it was extremely noisy. I didn't get much sleep that night. I just wanted to go home and sleep in my own bed. I was released to go home a few days later with a lot of pain medications. I remember being home and feeling so much pain I actually fainted a few times, and my dad took me to the emergency room just to make sure I was fine. During this time, I lost twenty pounds.

Summer was coming to an end. It would soon be time to for me to go and register for school. I was still enrolled at Temple City High and my registration date was near. When I came back from camp, my spirit was different. All I wanted to do was be in church. I had a desire to be in the presence of God and fellowship with all the new people I met. So, I started to go to Family Life Center Apostolic Church in Whittier on Friday nights, since my church didn't have services on that night.

My mom and dad said cancer made me a better person.

I remember school registration came and I had to register, but something was different. I felt like maybe I shouldn't go back to Temple City. I was happy to see my old friends, but after leaving I went home, and I started to think and fear came upon me. I was afraid if I went back, I wouldn't be an influence on people, but that people would be influencing me like they did in the years before. I was ashamed of being the "good kid." I felt like I had to fit in and go to all the football games on Friday nights. When people asked me, "Why do you wear skirts? How come you don't wear pants?" I just replied, "Because that's my style, I like to be different." I didn't want to lie about who I was anymore. I was done with being ashamed. I knew that I was better than that because God had brought me out of sin. My dad noticed when he took me to register that I was quiet, so he used that time to talk to me about the choices that I had made before and the new choices I was going to have to make for myself as a young woman of God. I told my dad that I wanted a new start and that I wanted to go to the private Apostolic school.

I felt no pressure from my parents. They left the ball in my hands and were waiting for my decision. In the meantime, I'm sure they were praying for direction for me.

Later that day, while talking to my mom, she mentioned that Family Life Center had a Christian private school, and if I wanted we could call and inquire about the school. I still wasn't sure. I decided to attend FLC my junior year and my senior year. I will graduate this year, super excited. My mom was surprised that I wanted to go, because she never thought I'd make the decision for myself. I knew it was for the best.

The Secretary of East LA Messengers of Peace, and Rebekah Hernandez, approached my parents at a district service. She asked how my recovery was going. My parents said I was great. She later invited me to share my testimony at a youth revival in Huntington Beach. Rev. Mingo Garcia would be the keynote speaker that day. I was honored and able to share the healing that took place in my body. I declared what the Lord did, and many young people who weren't at youth camp were able to hear my testimony. After sharing my testimony at the revival, I've had several opportunities to speak about what the Lord has done. I was invited on the IHAT testimony with Rev. Mario Naraja. It's a podcast that shares testimonies and airs on The Fountain App that plays Apostolic preachings, teachings, and testimonies. Later, I was invited to El Monte Apostolic Church to share with the ladies and young girls. Apostolic Jubilee was great! It was another platform to let everyone know that God is in the healing business. I spoke at Community Hope church and I served as a staff member at juniors camp for East LA District. I was able to sing, and it was honestly such a blessing because God was using me. Everyone knows I was the girl who HAD cancer.

I recently went to the Apostolic Convention in Long Beach. I saw a lot of familiar faces, one being my very good friend, Mingo Garcia, and his wife. They were both pleased to see the young woman of God that I've become. Mingo was stationed at a booth for International Missions. Alongside him was Bishop Andy Provencio, the Secretary of International Missions. Mingo began to ask the bishop if he had heard my testimony. The bishop was blown away and mentioned that I should go on a missionary trip when I turn eighteen. They both said that my testimony could heal an entire village.

My life has changed dramatically. I am more involved in church. I serve God because I have my own relationship with Him. I am so thankful for the journey God took me on, and I know He is a healer and nothing is impossible for Him.

Contac information for speaking engagements:
Uniqueangel2001@gmail.com

Ryan with Mom & Dad

Praying at the Accident

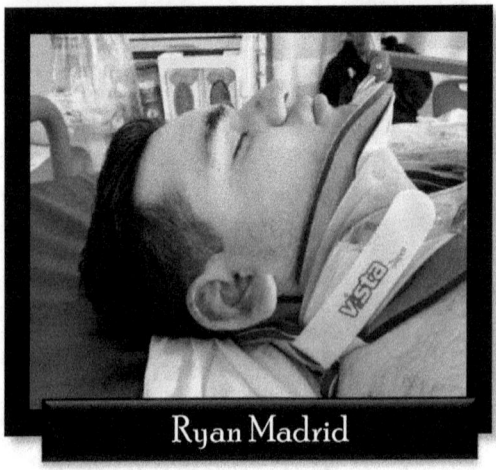
Ryan Madrid

CHAPTER 6

Renie Madrid

It was cold and rainy. The clock struck 4:00 pm, and another school day had ended. Not yet time to leave, as we were a one-vehicle family, my two boys, my daughter and I needed to wait to get picked up after Dad and the older brothers were off work. With an hour of waiting, we usually did homework. But on this particular Wednesday, my nephew Andrew, a fellow student, walked in class announcing that he was leaving with his dad (my brother-in-law, Rev. Nathan Cupoli) to get a haircut. My mind started clicking: "My boys need a haircut too," "If I send them to get a haircut, I will NOT have to give the haircut myself and be covered with hair," and "This barber is inexpensive."

The next thing out of my mouth was, "Andrew wait... I'm gonna send my boys with you and your dad!" I shoved money in my boys' hands and off they went to the corner. Outside, it was only drizzling. Boys being boys, they decided to make an adventure out of it and walk the two blocks.

Around forty-five minutes later, still in my classroom, I heard the horrible screeching scream of my sister, "Reeennieee!" The sound of panic and desperation in her voice told me there was something incredibly wrong.

I yelled back, "What?"

"Ryan has been hit by a car!"

I instantly felt as if I had been directly punched in my stomach and my head went in a blinding spin. I ran outside, where a friend had her car waiting for me. Driving only two blocks felt like forever, yet I felt as if I were thinking of a hundred things at the same time. I was not able to get a hold of my husband, due to the bad cell reception where he worked. What was I going to find? All I could do was start to pray. Was our son dead? Dying? Crippled? Experiencing permanent damage?

We pulled up and I jumped out of the car. I could see my son lying on the wet pavement, not moving. There were people around, the car and driver that hit him and spectators in the vehicles from the traffic jam caused by the accident. As I was running towards him, so many things were running through my mind. "How can I live my life without my son?" "Is this the last time I'm going to see him?" "Will he be crippled for life?" The fear was absolutely gripping. I knelt beside him and he was completely unconscious. I wasn't sure if he was even alive. I needed to check if he was breathing.

The rain was really coming down and I used my body to shield the rain from his face. I was afraid to move him. A few moments later the ambulance arrived, police were on scene, and I could hear people crying and praying. Then I heard the most amazing sound. I heard my son softly cry and say, "Mom." The sheer relief changed my frantic crying to sobbing. I was so grateful that the Lord brought my son back to me. However, I knew he wasn't out of the woods. We were not sure of the injuries that he had. He was experiencing pain, but he was also still in shock. As of today, he has no memory of this time. They put him on the stretcher, everyone crying, everyone praying, standing in the rain on that corner. Finally, we were off to the hospital now.

Emergency rooms are scary, and even more so when it's your loved one needing the care. The ambulance driver informed me that we were going to a hospital that had specialists. According to the EMT driver, my son had experienced injuries that required the specialists. Emergency room doctors ran many tests on Ryan. After several hours, the doctors came in and explained to my husband and me that Ryan had a fracture to his skull and that the artery near the left side of his brain was bleeding. He explained that if the bleeding persisted, they would need to drill a hole in his skull near the artery to relieve the pressure.

As scary as this all was, even then we knew God was already performing miracles. Doctors were already amazed that my son had not experienced any broken bones, other than his skull. The doctor was going to perform a test every three hours to monitor whether Ryan's brain continued to bleed. This would determine whether he would need to have major surgery. The first test wasn't good, in that the bleeding persisted. We continued to pray, and by the time the next three hours had passed, the bleeding had stopped and major surgery would not be required.

Once the doctors decided major surgery was not needed, we were in recovery time. Ryan was in the pediatrics ICU, and they were monitoring him. Seeing my son chilling, eating, in good spirits and responding well made us all question whether this was as bad an accident as we had originally thought. After all, neither my husband nor I were there when our son got hit. Perhaps all our fears were exaggerated. We were just simply happy that our son was doing well. Only forty-eight hours after being hit by a car, Ryan was leaving the hospital. We were given instructions to take him to a follow-up appointment with his primary doctor within two days.

This was an awesome visit, going to see his new primary pediatrician. Apparently, she received all our paperwork from the emergency room prior to coming into our room. She read through all the descriptions of his injuries and how he obtained them. She walked in and looked perplexed. She asked Ryan questions such as, "How do you feel?" and "Explain to me again what happened to you?" So, Ryan and I explained how he obtained the injuries from this hit, and her response was great. She said "I'm looking at you, I am looking at the injuries that you've obtained, and it doesn't make sense. I have kids coming to my office who have had more severe symptoms from being hit in the head with a soccer ball than what you are experiencing, it just doesn't make sense."

So I, his mother, proceeded to ask her a question: "Are you saying that you're surprised that my son doesn't have more severe symptoms?"

She replied with a resounding, "Yes, that's what I'm saying. My nurses read all the paperwork and give me a briefing on what I should expect before I walk in and see a patient. I also read through the report given to me regarding all of his injuries and I was nervous about coming in because of the severity of what he's been through. I didn't know what I was walking in to see. And here you are, looking like you are completely fine. It just doesn't make sense."

Ryan and I were looking at each other, smiling. I looked at the doctor and said, "Well, my family and I have many people praying and we believe that when it doesn't make sense, it's God! This is a God thing! At first, I was thinking that perhaps he didn't have such severe injuries, but you're telling me that it was that serious and that this is a miracle, correct? Is that what you're saying?"

She replied with, "Yes, I'd have to agree with you."

I couldn't believe she admitted it! We were so happy, my son and I just smiled at each other.

Hearing this from the doctor confirmed that the Lord had His hand over my son. The following Sunday after coming home from the hospital, we decided to take my nephew out for his birthday. He was one of the family members walking with my son when he was hit by the car, and we thought taking them out for dinner would be a celebration of everyone being healthy and protected by the Lord. While standing on the corner where this traumatic event had taken place, we noticed a security camera on a building. We reached out to the owner and obtained video footage of the accident. This video highlighted and shone a spotlight on the Lord's hand and the miracle that this truly was.

Miracles are not just occurrences of days gone by. Miracles are still happening today.

Contac information for speaking engagements: Fredreniemadrid@gmail.com

Esther Zazueta

Wedding Day

40 Years Later

CHAPTER 7

Esther Zazueta

My name is Esther Zazueta and I live in Tucson, AZ. I am blessed with fifteen grandchildren and three great sons: Elias, Benjamin, and Peter. My husband, Willie and I have now been married forty-five years.

With so much testosterone challenging my life, the Lord sent me an angel in the form of my daughter-in-law, Monique. She is the daughter I never had. As my boys were growing up, my husband played men's fast pitch softball, which took him away from the boys and me. Fridays came along and Willie would be out the door to play wherever the wind blew. At that time, Benjamin and Peter were playing baseball as well. For Willie, that meant more time with the team playing, drinking, and doing drugs. My boys and I would notice the difference in Willie's personality when spending time away from home. I would tell the boys that wasn't their dad, but the drugs and alcohol taking over. Sad to say, we would get happy when he would leave for the weekend. That way he could go and come as he pleased without causing a ruckus at home. At the time Willie didn't think he was wrong in how he was living, but it put a lot of stress on the rest of the family. Between working two jobs, I would make sure the boys went to school and baseball practice and for the most part stay out of trouble. I worked at a sorority house as a cook from 6am to 2pm, and then the deli at Kmart from 3pm to close at 11pm. I worked two jobs because my husband had hurt his back and didn't work for two years.

I would never say anything negative about my husband because I was taught that my marriage was for better or worse. Don't get me wrong, my husband was a great guy, but when he was with his friends drinking and doing drugs, we weren't even a close second. It was as if I and the kids didn't exist. At that time, we were not going to church. I worked two jobs and did my house chores on my day off, making sure my boys had everything they needed for the week. My three boys went to church, and one night my son Peter was baptized without our consent. My father, who was a minister, gave permission for him to get baptized. We were hurt because we wanted to be there and make sure he understood what he was getting himself into.

My mother always taught me not to let go of God's hand. I know that it was my mom's and dad's prayers as well as my in-laws that kept me and my boys safe. Willie's mom and dad always prayed that he would return to God.

Willie was like that black sheep of the family, and when I say black, I mean pitch black. One day I asked God what I could do to change our situation because I could not live the way we were living much longer.

Shortly after that prayer, Peter was then drafted by the St. Louis Cardinals baseball team, receiving a good signing bonus. At the time, Elias was out of the house and Benjamin had gotten married, giving us our first grandchild. With that signing bonus, Peter moved us to Merced, California, in hopes of getting my husband delivered. James, a member of the Merced church, came to pray for him, and God delivered him. I know God had His hands over us. You see, God does answer prayer in His time.

I met George Pantages when my husband and I lived in Merced. We lived there for two years, and I also met Tim, his son. They would come over for dinner and we became like family. We moved away, and so did Brother Pantages, and we were in his wedding a short time later. He married Maria, a lovely person with a sweet spirit. We moved back to Tucson, Arizona, where we now congregate with Pastor Connor. Tucson has always been home to us.

As soon as we settled in, I found a job as a cook for a sorority house at the University of Arizona. I worked for twenty-one years as a cook and then became a house director for two sorority houses. I worked seven years for one house and three years at the other. When I worked at the sorority house, I would see how different things were from the time that I cooked for them. Young ladies were scantily dressed, not to mention the disrespectful language when they spoke to their parents. The drinking, the partying, not really caring about themselves really broke my heart. One of my girls, who I was concerned about, was having problems with anxiety because her parents had gotten a divorce. Then her father met someone and was going to get married, and her new stepmother was not going to pay her college tuition anymore. So, she was acting out. She would take pills to study until she could not live without them. I talked to her about getting help, which was going out on a limb, because as a house mom we were not to get involved. But my heart went out to her and I helped her the best I could. I would make sure the cook had left food when she came home late.

I can truly say she is better now. She has a 4.0 GPA and she recently thanked me for praying for her. She now believes God put us together and is thankful He did. I hear from her every once in a while, and she is doing fine. Her grandparents help her now with her tuition and she works two jobs.

In 2018, my husband and I were going to be on spring break for a week. We were getting ready to go see my family in California. But one morning I was not feeling good. My stomach felt like it was bloated, and I couldn't catch my breath, so I called my doctor and explained how I was feeling. He told me to go to the hospital to get checked out, and I did. The next thing I knew, they were taking fluid out of my stomach, which amounted to about four liters of fluid. They sent me home with an appointment to see a doctor at a cancer center. Of course, I was worried, so my son Peter and Monique and my husband went to the appointment with me. We went into the doctor's office and waited what seemed like an eternity. The doctor came in and told us that I had cancer. We were quiet, and I could see tears in my husband's eyes and in Monique's as well. Peter didn't let me see his emotions, playing the tough guy, but I knew deep down inside he was hurting more than all of us put together. He and I have a kindred spirit so to speak, we are both spiritually gifted, and that has created a bond I do not have with any of my other sons.

When I caught my composure, I said, "Okay, what stage is the cancer in?" and the doctor said stoically, "Stage 4." I was speechless. I asked how long I had, and the doctor said about six months. They could run tests to see what treatments they could do. I felt so numb and really didn't know what was going to happen. As a mother, your mind starts racing 100 miles an hour, thinking of any and every possibility in the short time I had left. What about my family, my husband, my grandchildren? My heart felt like it cracked in half and was oozing all over the place.

We went home to let my son Elias and the grandchildren know, and of course they all cried. I started to think how the in world was I going to tell my family in California and Texas? So, we decided to take a trip to California to let my family know. I called my sister so they could get my family together. It was my sister's birthday, and so getting together was no problem. When I finally got the nerve to tell them what was going on, there were tears and hugs, but my family rallied together and they said they would be praying for me and help me any way they could. When my siblings get together, we show our love for one another, no holds barred.

When we got back to Arizona, Peter called different cancer clinics. He found one in Phoenix, AZ, so he made an appointment. It was about that time Peter and Monique had some church friends come and have dinner at their home. Well, on this night there were about four families sitting at the table and my son asked the family to pray for me in a circle and they did. It was an awesome prayer. Shortly after that, I went back to work, because I lived at the sorority house. My son had called Brother Pantages to tell him that I had Stage 4 cancer. Then I got a phone call from Brother Pantages, saying he felt led to come pray for me in person. He and his wife Maria drove twenty-four hours straight from Texas just to pray for me. They came to Peter's house, but before he prayed, he prophesied that at the time of the prayer I would vomit up whatever was bothering me on the inside. Sure enough, as he laid hands on me, I began to vomit up whatever was inside my stomach. He then took some time to go to each member of the family and prophesy over them as well. The glory of God filled the room, and no one was excluded that day from feeling the merciful hand of God. The Lord also included a family friend who was prophesied over as well. God truly left no stone unturned that day.

    I know God healed me that day. I felt so special that God would send a man of God to pray for me. But then he and Sister Maria drove back the same day to Texas. I still kept the appointment in Phoenix at the Mayo Clinic and talked to the doctor. She knew what I had but she wanted to run tests just to be sure. So, she did blood work and a CTC scan. I came back a week later and was hoping the doctor would not find anything. But that day they put a port where they take out blood, meaning they were preparing me for chemo treatments. My blood count didn't look good, so that day they started chemo. I cried because I really didn't want to start chemo. I called my son and asked him if I should do this. I felt like I was letting God down, knowing I was healed. But my son said that was why there were doctors: to help us when our faith ran low.

    My doctors knew just what I had and how to treat it, so I did chemo for twelve weeks every Monday. My family would wait four hours each time I went. So, I prayed "God, if this is Your will, please help me get through this." I thank God that I did not get sick like other people I saw when they got negative reactions from their treatments. I initially had a lot of energy that would run out mid-week. Occasionally, my husband would take me for my treatment, but usually it was one of my sons. We were in this thing together. Why? Because we were family. Peter would make me laugh, because with chemo I was losing my hair and I would wear knitted hats. Clowning around he would put it on the way, driving me to my appointment. We would then listen to gospel music, which made the drive so much faster.

I was told I had peritoneal cancer, which is a rare cancer. It develops in a thin layer of tissue that lines the abdomen. It also covers the uterus, bladder, and rectum. I did the treatments and then had surgery that took four hours. My husband was there with some close friends of ours, including his brother who flew in from Louisiana.

When they did the surgery, they also took out my spleen and sent it to the lab. When it came back, it was filled with cancer. The spleen is there to help fight infections, so now without it I would have to be taking shots to help me fight infections. After surgery, I went to a hotel to rest before going home. That night I asked my husband to comb my hair. He looked at me and said he was sorry, but my hair fell out with the comb. I knew I would lose my hair, but I didn't want to lose all of it. Of course, I kind of cried, and to add to my problems, the chemo caused neuropathy in my feet, which caused a lot of pain, not to mention feeling extremely cold.

At the same time, my husband had surgery to treat diverticulitis (which can cause severe abdominal pain, fever, nausea and a marked change in your bowel habits).

If that was not enough, my daughter-in-law had surgery to remove her gallbladder. One thing after the other, the hits just kept on coming. I asked the Lord what was going on and to please help us get through this difficult time. Yes, I cried and asked God to help, but I would cry away from family because I wanted to be strong for them. It was difficult, because when Brother Pantages prayed for me, he said that I would have to let go trying to do so much for my children. I was being more of a peacekeeper than a peacemaker, to the detriment of my family. Let me tell you, it's hard. I would ask God to give me strength. I prayed for my loved ones in my family who are still unsaved, hoping that my example would help them see how great and mighty is the God I serve. All I ever wanted was for others to see what God has done for me. Through this whole ordeal, I never realized so many people I didn't even know were praying for me. So many people in our local church took the time to touch God's throne in my behalf and I could feel their prayers. You don't realize how many people are praying for you, but I sure could feel it.

    My job has been so good to me in that the ladies in the sorority were ready to help me with many things I would normally do around the house before I got sick. After the sixth week of chemo, we saw my doctor and she let me know that I didn't have to do chemo anymore. So, my husband and I asked her, "What does that mean?" She said with a smile, "No more cancer."

    I was cancer-free. Well, I didn't know whether to cry, run, or jump. But those words made me happy. The doctor said to go celebrate. We left, called my family, and cried in the car. I left a message for my pastor as well. You see, sometimes you still have to go through things to build someone's faith, or by showing them that God loved me enough to heal me, He loves them enough to hear their prayer. God is so awesome!!!

Daniel & Jasmin Torres

Micah & Dad

Micah & Mom

The Rest of the Clan

CHAPTER 8

Daniel & Jasmin Torres

If you ever meet my husband, Daniel, you will quickly find out he is a storyteller. He was raised by a single mom, living from house to house all of his childhood life. The safest haven was his grandparent's home, and his grandpa had been the only father figure he knew. His stories come from the childhood he experienced and how he came to know God through his grandpa. I, on the other hand, was raised in church with both parents. The only life I knew was growing in a Christian (Apostolic) atmosphere. At the time my husband and I met, he was a redeemed alcoholic, helping raise twin boys. I had come out of an abusive marriage and was a single mom, raising a daughter. Our childhoods had been extremely different, but the love we each carried as parents brought us together. Six years into our marriage, we had grown from having three to having six. Our blended family had already been exposed to many differences and disappointments. We had had numerous counseling sessions with different counselors, but their efforts were unsuccessful. Dealing with my anxiety and residue of postpartum depression didn't seem to help the situation very much. My son Micah had been a huge surprise upon his arrival (2014). My husband and I had decided that once our son turned one, we would go our separate ways.

I remember pleading with God during this time, "Lord, will You just intervene!" I'm sure my husband was feeling the same way, but no matter how much we tried, we weren't getting anywhere. There was no doubt that God had put us together, but the odds of being a blended family had always been against us since the beginning.

During the winter season, our Micah had been in out of the emergency room. We were sent home every single time with what seemed to only be an upper respiratory problem. We were already into the new year (2015), and Micah was still taking trips to the ER. One day while giving Micah a bath, I noticed his stomach was very hard and bloated. I thought maybe he was experiencing bowel movement difficulties. Then from one week to another, we began to notice a lump on the right side of his stomach. Every week it got bigger and more noticeable. We weren't taking as much trips to the emergency room, but my mother instinct knew something just wasn't right. I finally decided to call his pediatrician, but because it was during business hours, the nurse had to return my phone call. I described to her Micah's stomach along with his symptoms. She reminded me that we had his one-year check-up in the next couple of weeks and just to mention it to the doctor during our visit. The week had gone by and I kept weighing my options of just taking him to the nearest emergency room. Saturday morning arrived and my dad stopped by. That morning I mentioned to my dad what was going on with Micah. He suggested we not ignore it and immediately take him to the ER. My husband agreed to take him, while I stayed back with our two toddlers (two and three) and our oldest daughter (twelve years at that time). The morning had gone by and I hadn't heard from my husband. I decided to text him and he replied, "Ultrasound." That evening my husband finally called me back. He was sighing, as though he had been crying with all his might.

"I need you to come quickly and meet me at the hospital, the ambulance is about to get here to transfer Micah to Texas Children's."

I suddenly felt like my heart had stopped beating and all the sounds around me faded as I tried to talk.

"Why, babe, but why, what happened!"

I could feel his tears on my end of the phone as he said, "The ultrasound images are showing he has a tumor growing. Babe, please hurry, please!"

I immediately hung up and began to pace back and forth. I recall my dad gathering my children and praying a prayer of peace and strength. The first words that came to me were, "The Lord is my light and my salvation; whom shall I fear? The Lord is the strength of my life, of who shall I be afraid?" (Psalm 27:1)

I finally arrived at our local hospital; they had just put my baby boy's car seat on the stretcher with him in it. My husband was sobbing in tears with desperation. As the ambulance drove from our local hospital to Texas

Children's Hospital, everything seemed so foggy in my mind, but the sound of my baby boy giggling kept my heart still. My husband was following the ambulance in our vehicle, and as he was driving he had a conversation with God. He reminded God of the life that he had before he gave his life to Him. Many times, he asked God to help him and God would answer. He would usually go right back to doing what was unacceptable in God's eyes. But at this point in his life it was different, my husband had been serving God for six years. He realized how hard it was to turn away from all sins of the world, but he did it in an act of obedience. He asked God in that moment, "Will You honor my obedience and heal my son? I changed six years ago for this moment!"

The ambulance had finally arrived at Texas Children's. My husband had worked there many years ago, but never thought his baby boy would be the one brought in through a stretcher. What happened from there on was truly orchestrated by God! We were escorted to our room, while in the lobby our family, friends, and our pastors were already waiting for us. One by one, they were allowed to enter the room, as the sound of prayer could be heard through the halls. Micah's first blood pressure reading was so high, the nurses couldn't understand his happy mood. Micah's little innocent heart was clueless to what was occurring at that very time. He showed no sign of being ill. The nurse walked back and said it would be hours until we would be escorted back for scans. Mind you, by that time, it was dark outside. I wasn't sure what to expect, but before even giving it much thought, a doctor walked in.

She said, "I will be taking care of you tonight," as she wrote her name on the dry erase board. My husband's jaw dropped. The chief doctor, who was very well known through TCH's television commercials, was giving the nurses instructions. She continued, "We are doing his scans right now and in less than twenty-four hours, we will have a plan for the care of your son!"

Suddenly a "peace that surpasses all understanding" took over our minds. It felt as though the "Great Physician" had walked in. At that very moment, we didn't have specific results nor an exact plan, but we had a reassurance that God was in control. I could see my husband's face begin to brighten up. Before we knew it, my husband was walking with our boy out into the hall for scans.

In the next twenty-four hours, everything happened so rapidly. Micah was transferred to the Intensive Care Unit to have his blood pressure monitored very closely. I will never forget the feeling of the first time I walked into that Intensive Care Unit. My assurance had gone to a level of uncertainty. As the hours passed by, the wires over Micah were accumulating very quickly. What happened that following morning, on a Sunday, was the beginning of heart-wrenching details that would forever be embedded in my mind. The area where Micah was located was closed in with a sliding-glass door. We could see a group of doctors and nurses gather in a circle, carefully looking at a computer screen. They walked my husband and me outside the glass doors.

The first doctor pointed at the screen and said, "This is what your son's kidney looks like...there is a tumor the size of an orange sitting on your son's right kidney." The doctor continued "...but there is also what seems to look like another small tumor growing on his left." The doctors all paused, waiting for me and my husband's reaction.

Not being so knowledgeable in the medical field and just thinking like a mom, I blurted it out, "Well can you just take it out?"

The next doctor responded, "It's not that simple." He explained that they didn't know the makeup of the tumor, and if the surgeon were to remove it, the tumor could burst. If it was malignant, the cancer could spread to other parts of his body. Suddenly there was a knot in my throat, while my husband broke down in tears, trying so hard to find his composure. The doctor finished by saying, "We are going to treat this as cancer, we will be coming up with a plan to treat this..."

Everything in my mind seemed so foggy again. That evening, the nurses asked us to step out, they would be sedating Micah to put in an artery line. We sat outside the room and for the first time since we had arrived, we heard our baby boy cry. His cries were so heartbreaking that my husband couldn't stand around any longer, he had to walk away. I had always been the stronger one in our marriage, and up until that point, I hadn't fully processed it all because I wanted to stay strong. I cried as I sat there and listened to the cries of my eleven-month-old baby boy. The artery line was unsuccessful, and Micah would have to be scheduled for anesthesia.

On March 10, 2015, my Facebook post that night ended like this: "...And as we wait for the doctors and surgeons to come up with a plan, we will continue to trust God in the process of Micah's healing, from the top of his head to the soles of his feet! There is no greater name than to call out on that sweet name 'Jesus' while waiting! Though a host should encamp against me, my heart shall not fear: though war should rise against me, in this will I be confident, Psalm 27:3." Our attitudes in that twenty-four-hour process had surely been the foundation of what was to come.

While in the ICU, we encountered many obstacles. The doctors and surgeons finally came up with a plan. The plan was that once Micah left the ICU, he would check into the cancer center on the ninth floor to begin his first chemotherapy. Once everything was fully assessed, he would go home and continue with weekly visitations for treatment, till the doctors re-evaluated. The only problem was that Micah's blood pressure was still elevated. In the meanwhile, Micah was put to sleep to have a port inserted. The various types of medicine for chemotherapy would be inserted through the port. I remember that as the days were passing by and getting closer to becoming a week, my husband and I became weary as our son was still in the Intensive Care Unit. We took turns staying with Micah throughout the day and night. here wasn't a place to sleep, except a chair that didn't recline. Our entire energy was being consumed and the enemy had found an open door. One night as I began to feel weary, no matter what I tried, I couldn't shake it off. And to top everything off, from left to right, patients had not been doing so well in the ICU. There were constant "CODE BLUE" announcements. It almost felt as though a spirit of death had entered in the ICU room that night.

I stepped out to call a dear friend of mine and began to tell her the heaviness that I was feeling. She said, "Jazmin, take out your oil and anoint the door of Micah's room." To others who were watching, this probably was the silliest thing, but my desperation pushed me to great measures.

Micah's blood pressure readings showed a significant change throughout the night. The next morning, the nurses were given the green light to start Micah's transfer to the ninth floor in the cancer center. Once again, we had seen the hand of God move!

The ninth floor was where all cancer patients stayed when they were admitted. We met children with their parents who had made this place their home. The severity of cancer had made it impossible for them to leave the hospital. The atmosphere was bitter-sweet, as my husband and I watched the faces of children smile in spite of their circumstances. Our stay on the ninth floor changed something in our hearts and minds forever. As we settled, the social worker walked us over to the infusion center. This would be the place where Micah would have his weekly chemotherapy once he was sent home. And this was the moment that I, as a mom, broke! The fact that my son had cancer had become my reality. I remember walking down the hall with the social worker, and I suddenly stopped with uncontrollable tears. I never knew this place existed, and I couldn't understand why God had chosen my son to be there. I suddenly had so many questions for God. Nevertheless, somewhere deep in my heart, I knew God wasn't going to forsake us.

The following evening, our Micah was scheduled for his first chemotherapy. We were warned of all the side effects that chemo would cause, such as drop foot syndrome, loss of vocal cords, and low immune system. That evening, my husband and I united in prayer that God would protect Micah from all the above. This was the beginning of many prayers throughout Micah's battle.

After being at the hospital for a week, we were finally sent home with a treatment plan for Micah. For the next six weeks, he would continue chemotherapy once a week. The doctors wanted to see if the tumors would shrink with the help of chemotherapy and if so, would it be a drastic change. Our storm wasn't over, but the waves had calmed enough to keep our heads above the waters. This new change to our home dynamics wasn't easy. Our children back at home had felt the absence of my husband and me. The little ones couldn't comprehend, and the older ones were lacking attention. Keeping everything as normal as possible was impossible. It was almost as though our world had been split into two and there was nothing we could do to change what lay ahead. In the next six weeks, we would be walking into the unknown, the uncertainties of not knowing what to expect. The enemy gave me constant reminders that my son had a tumor and the doctors in all reality didn't know whether it was malignant or benign.

One morning as I was out in my flower garden, a spirit of fear came over me. I began to think, "What if God chooses not to heal my son and what if I lose my baby boy?" I decided to call my dear friend to help me sort my emotions. She reminded me that all my years of living and walking with God had come down to this moment of faith. These words brought me back to my knees, to the very place I had prayed months ago for God to intervene in our home. As I was on my knees, I wrestled with the thoughts of fear, death, and loss. And then the word of God came to me, "Though I walk through the valley of the shadow of death, I will fear no evil." Never had this scripture made sense to me, but that day, I was in that valley and death was a reality. I cried before God with all my soul and might, "Lord, I surrender my will to Yours, my Micah belongs to You, but will You please spare me my son?" I poured my heart out to God, as I refused to get up without an answer. That morning God gave me three words, "IT IS DONE!" These three words would be my reminder as we stood in the battlefield.

The Heartbreak Mender 2

Four weeks into Micah's chemotherapy, the team of doctors decided that our son would be scheduled to have surgery. We were told that Micah's tumor on the right was slightly shrinking, but the chemotherapy was having no effect on the one on the left, and it was diagnosed as "pre-stage." Well, a week before surgery, Micah spiked a fever and it was protocol to take him in to be examined. We rushed him to the ER, where he was admitted to the tenth floor for a blood transfusion. Our Micah's ANC counts were at 130. He was fighting with no immune system. He needed breathing treatments every four hours. That night, my heart was on the floor as I watched my son fight for his life. Our prayers were changing by the hour, and once again our God moved as we counted the small victories of Micah slowly gaining his immune system back.

The doctors wouldn't let us go home until Micah's ANC reached 500. A day turned into a week. My husband was drained between work, home and our stay at the hospital. Staying on the tenth floor was the most uncomfortable setting. Since the ninth floor gave us access to our everyday necessities, it made it more like home. Micah's room was located at the very end of the hall, past double doors, and our view out the window was of another building. I realized in the middle of my frustration that we had gotten too comfortable in the valley, we lost sight of the victories in front of us. That Friday, we had a visit from a couple from our church, a minister and his wife. I knew they were there to visit my son, but that day I was in desperate need of prayers. I really believe that God had provided someone to pour into my soul. That morning before they left, God renewed my spirit with a new praise in my mouth. That same day, Micah reached the 500 mark in his ANC, the doctor discharged him to go home and we were scheduled to be right back the next week for surgery.

The day of surgery finally arrived and the people who would take part on this day were truly orchestrated by God, just like the day we walked into the ER. My husband held our son tight as we walked Micah to get prepped for surgery. He began to cry as we waited for the team of doctors and nurses to take our son. My husband needed words of assurance more than I did. Right before the nurses started the anesthesia process, the same minister and wife who had visited with us the week before rushed over to where we were. They reminded my husband of the story of Moses, how his mother put him in a basket not knowing what to expect. Jochebed, the mother of Moses, trusted that God would protect him from all the dangers in the waters. Even though she couldn't see what lay ahead, she kept her faith in God. These words of comfort were a Godsend, just like every other time God had sent the right person at the right time. They prayed over our Micah before he was put in the hands of surgeons, doctors and nurses.

As we waited back in the waiting area with our family and friends, we were given updates from a medical assistant appointed to Micah's surgery. It wasn't required for him to give us updates every hour, but by this thoughtful gesture, we knew God had appointed him. We were finally told that Micah was in the recovery room. But before seeing our boy, we sat with the surgeon to get all the details of Micah's surgery. We were told that the doctor who performed Micah's surgery was a renowned surgeon. There was no doubt that God had aligned us with the very best. The surgeon began by telling us how the surgery was a success, but it was unfortunate that the right kidney had to be removed along with the tumor. What had been seen on Micah's scans and diagnosed as "pre-stage" on the left, was a very tiny cyst: It wasn't cancer! Before surgery, the doctor had mentioned that if the right kidney was removed, the adrenal gland would have to come with it. Well, Micah was able to keep the adrenal gland because there weren't any attachments. When that very tiny cyst was wedged out on the left kidney, the surgeon said he had also been concerned about having to put in a drain line, but thankfully the drain line wasn't needed at all. The surgeon did a sectioning of lymph nodes for any possible spreads. If the results tested positive, Micah would need radiation on the target area, but if it tested negative, Micah would only need chemo. There was a very slim chance that the tumor removed on the right would be considered malignant. Though the doctors could not confirm biopsy results yet, in our eyes God had already done the miraculous. After a couple of hours in the recovery room, the nurses felt like Micah was ready to be placed in a room. To our surprise, it wasn't the cancer center on the ninth floor, nor the tenth, but it was on the eleventh floor that our Micah would finish his recovery. Because our Micah was never again admitted to the ninth floor, we couldn't ignore these small details. And just like we had learned to walk out of our comfort zone while being on the tenth floor, we knew that our stay on the eleventh floor was one step closer to our son's miracle.

After a week of staying at the hospital, we were scheduled to meet with the surgeon for results two weeks later. We were told that the tumor Micah had was a "favorable tumor," exactly what the team of doctors had hoped for. The tumor was encapsulated, meaning it was benign. And it was located on the outer edges of the kidney, barely touching it. Therefore, the Wilms's Tumor was diagnosed as a Stage 2. All thirty-plus lymph nodes samples came back negative, but Micah would have to continue chemotherapy. This would be done as a precautionary measure to make sure there weren't any cells left in those invisible places. The chemotherapy would be spread out over twenty weeks, taking breaks in between. As my husband and I soaked in all the details, our tears began to overflow. Our hearts were overwhelmed with joy, but Micah still didn't have the "all clear" signal. As weeks turned into months, we encountered many obstacles. Our Micah was rushed to the ER many times because of high fevers. There was a point in this phase that chemo had to be completely stopped. The chemotherapy was affecting Micah's vocal cords, making his voice hoarse. As we took a longer break, that meant his scheduled treatments would be pushed back further, making the process longer. Yet, we counted the victories along the way, Micah never experienced drop foot syndrome like the doctors said he would. In fact, he surprised us and learned how to walk.

Finally, our Micah was scheduled for his last treatment of chemotherapy. As a cancer patient, "ringing the bell" is a sign that you are now in remission. On September 17, 2015, our Micah rang the bell! We believe God gave our Micah the victory a long time ago, even before he "rang the bell," but on this day he was officially "cancer-free"!

Our hearts were grateful that our son was "cancer free," but we were still fighting the emotions of anxiety as our son continued to have scans every three months. Recently we were excited because it was the year (2018) Micah would go from having scans every three months to every six months. But in that visit, scans revealed a spot on his right lung. We later returned in three months, only for scan results to show that he also had a spot in his left lung. That night I sat in a parking lot with a heaviness over me, I suddenly remembered my prayer three years ago, where the enemy had tried to instill fear in me. I felt a spirit of boldness come over me as I prayed, "Lord, I surrender my will to Your will. If You are for us, then who shall be against us? If it is Your will for my Micah to go through this again, I know that You will never leave us nor forsake us. If You did it once, you will do it again! And that which You have started, you will finish!" I wanted the enemy to hear me, because this time he wasn't going to steal the three words God had given me then: "IT IS DONE"!

To make the story short, Micah was up for scans again. The nurse calls me a day before to tell me Micah had no insurance coverage. She suggested I could either pay out of pocket or wait till coverage started again. But it would still have to have doctor approval if we chose to wait, only because what was showing on the last scans. My husband and I couldn't understand why there was no insurance coverage, it had just been confirmed the week before and we certainly didn't have the money. We immediately began to pray. The nurse called us back the next day to tell us the doctor had approved for his scans to not be done until December. We knew right away that it had been of God for him to approve it.

The day had finally come for our Micah to have scans redone. As soon as the doctor walked in, she immediately said, "Guess what? Micah is moving up! He is going from three months to every six months! His scans are clear!"

As we stood in the gap for our Micah and walked into unfamiliar ground, there were times that it seemed as though God was silent. In those times, we learned to shift our prayers, even if they were constantly changing by the hour. Every prayer was a shift of God's hand aiming toward our fight, and every shift was one step closer to Micah's victory. God had allowed our world to be shaken so that HE could build a stronger foundation for our family. My husband knew who God was through the eyes of his grandpa, but didn't know what God could do for him. As for me, I knew who God was, but hadn't learned to completely trust Him.

In the course of time, our family has faced many obstacles, but our unshakeable faith has triumphed over them all!

Contac information for speaking engagements:
Jazmin_torres@att.net

The Goodwin Family

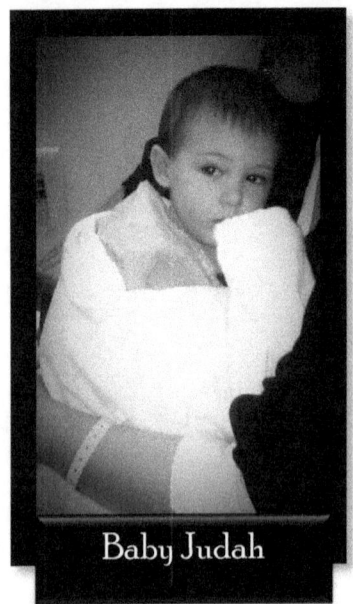

Baby Judah

Judah Goodwin

CHAPTER 9

Andrew & Tamara Goodwin

We open our story in February 2012, with my husband and I at the doctor's office, waiting for our sonogram results.

Andrew: It was one of those days, thinking life was good, God was blessing. I had officially become pastor of a church several months prior, all my family was living around the area, and another baby boy was on the way.

Tamara: I always said I loved my two sons and I just wanted to be blessed with another healthy child. However, the real moment of truth came when I found myself sobbing after we were just informed that our third child would be another son. I realized I had been lying to God and to myself. After my mom's passing, about six months earlier, I had secretly wanted a daughter to continue with the mother-daughter bond I had been blessed with growing up. After leaving the doctor's office, my husband and I headed back to our family's house where we were expected for dinner. That was where our two children would already be waiting for us while typically being spoiled by the family.

Andrew: We were outside talking with some of our family members. Our sons were playing around in the grass. (Something rare for us, since living in the desert.) Soon the truck of a family member came driving up the long driveway where we were standing. My wife and I both made sure the boys were out of the way, and then allowed them to go back to playing once the truck was stopped. (We had thought.)

Tamara: We were standing outside in the yard, discussing the turn of events from that day. As we were speaking, one of our younger family members came driving up the long driveway in a large four-wheel-drive Toyota pickup truck. I reached out to pick up my youngest son, Judah. (He was two years old at the time.) I held him until the truck had passed by, then immediately set him back down. My belly had grown so much that I could only carry him for short periods of time. That would become one of the most regretted actions of my life. The other kids were playing off to the left of the yard and were waving to the driver. The driver steered the truck to park to the right along with the other vehicles.

Andrew: However, the driver moved the vehicle, turning it into a spot to be further out of way. With excitement, Judah ran over to greet the driver, but failed to be noticed. I turned just as the truck knocked him down and ran over him, right before my eyes. It happened so fast but seemed like an eternity. I could not believe what I was seeing. My yelling seemed to land on deaf ears. I was thinking, "God, don't let Judah be dead! Let him be okay."

Tamara: As many of our family members stood there in the beauty of the day, it turned into horror as we watched my youngest son come from around another car, running up to meet that beloved family member. As the truck turned into the parking area, we watched in agony as the truck pushed him down and rolled over his body, from his lower abdomen to his groin and upper left thigh. In one swift moment, my world stopped, and it was as if I were watching a dramatic scene being played out in front of me. I remember trying to scream but felt like nothing was coming out because I didn't have enough air in my lungs. It literally took my breath away. We all started running to my boy. He wore an intense look of shock and fear, but he was not crying or moving. Then my ears opened to sounds around me. I heard everyone around me screaming and crying out to God. Pleading on that name above all names. The Name of JESUS!

Andrew: We rushed over to where he lay, not moving, but instead wide-eyed and in shock. Fear struck me hard! But I suppressed it because my son needed me. I had always been there for my boys. Their daddy would always be there to protect them.

Tamara: Movement at the truck caught my eye. The young driver was getting out of the truck, asking what was wrong. They heard the yelling and saw everyone's reactions. The driver had not felt the impact of the little body under the large truck. We were all in such a state of shock, when I was calling 911, the family couldn't remember their house address for the emergency operator.

Andrew: My brother-in-law wanted to take Judah inside, but I was unsure if we should move him. He understood my concern and we cautiously took Judah inside the house. Judah started to cry and scream as we laid him on the kitchen table and proceeded to cut his clothes away to better see the trauma to his body. It seemed like mere moments when the EMTs came rushing into the house. They wanted me to follow them to the hospital, but I was adamant about not leaving Judah's side. I informed them I would be riding with my son.

Tamara: My brother-in-law was quick with response and actions. He immediately started checking my son's body for apparent injuries and bleeding. Then he and my husband carried my son into the house to start cutting his clothes off to evaluate the injuries as best they could. Meanwhile, I ran to the front of the property to open the gate for the emergency crew. It felt like a long time, but in reality it took mere minutes to hear the sounds of the fire truck and ambulance approaching. Once the emergency crew arrived, I was told my sister-in-law would drive me while my husband rode in the ambulance with our son. Soon they would be leaving in route to the hospital.

Andrew: In the ambulance, on the way to the children's hospital, the EMT was constantly checking on Judah's vitals. His expressions and the terms he was using concerned me. I had been singing to Judah, "Jesus Loves Me," and stopped to ask questions. Every time I stopped singing, Judah would start screaming and crying. So I kept singing to Judah and he would stop screaming. There were multiple times I swallowed hard, trying to sing "Jesus Loves Me," when the thoughts going through my mind said, "How can He?"

Tamara: Looking back, I couldn't tell you what time of day this occurred, but in my memories of the car ride to the hospital, it was very dark outside. I remember no daylight. I remember feeling helpless and knew I was experiencing new levels of emotional distress unlike any I had experienced before. Distraught with the intensities of my emotions, I knew I couldn't pray the prayers my son was in desperate need of at that moment. I started frantically scrolling through my phone contacts to find anyone I knew who could and would stop to intercede. I was desperate for people to approach the throne of God on my son's behalf, right now! The first person I called was my grandpa, Paul C. Seagraves. A man of God, he had lived and preached precious Pentecostal truth without compromise. My calling was not a regular habit, so he answered happy to hear from me, but when he asked how I was doing I had to be honest. I gave him a briefing on the situation, but I remember saying, "Grandpa, I need people that can pray!! Please pray and call on the family for prayer! Please!!" He agreed and we hung up.

The next contact I made was via text. It was to a mighty seasoned woman of God who had given me her phone number when my mom passed, Sis. Mary Wilson. I had not had any intention of contacting her, but in this moment of desperation, I sent her a very brief but pleading text to pray. She responded and would also have their local church body pray during their service later that evening. Once I knew there would be people praying, I started crying and asking God to forgive me for not wanting this pregnancy to be another boy. I loved my sons and didn't want Him to take my little Judah from me or cause him harm because of my selfish motives earlier in the day.

Andrew: As we pulled up to the hospital, the ambulance doors opened, and I was surprised to see such a large crowd of doctors, nurses and staff. All waiting for our little boy, Judah to arrive. I didn't recall how many people were working on Judah, but they kept me at his head and in his ear, singing. It was quite amazing even to the doctors that as long as I kept singing to Judah, he would not scream. Yet it was obvious that he was in excruciating pain and was traumatized.

Tamara: To our dismay, somehow our car arrived at the hospital before the ambulance carrying my son and husband. I was asking and inquiring about their status when we were informed that the hospital ER Department was on alert and they were all ready and waiting for my son's arrival with a large crew to start working. That was not an exaggeration. There were three ER doctors/surgeons, about twenty ER nursing staff and six to eight administrative staff in that blocked-off quadrant, ready for the arrival of a two-year-old who had just been run over.

The status update given to me that night brought me to the realization just how critical this situation was. Once I heard the yells announcing the arrival of the expected patient, my mind started racing. I hadn't spoken to my husband since the moment of the accident, due to the need for action. There was no time for emotional support. There were so many staff on hand that I was barely able to see my husband's head pass by and failed to see my son. During the process, I had agreed to handle all the administrative paperwork and answer the hundred questions that come with trips to the ER, plus the additional hundred when the injured one is a minor. I was then informed that police were also dispatching their personnel to fill out an incident report.

While answering the questions and signing the paperwork, we were interrupted with the screams of my son. I stopped to demand a status update. I couldn't finish or even think clearly to answer more questions until I had answers myself. They tried very hard to reassure me that my Judah was in good hands and they would know more soon. That happened two or three times, until finally I couldn't take it or go on. The cries came so fast and strong and then stopped just as instantly as they came. Finally, a lady stepped through the busy crowd to speak with me.

She said, "I wanted to let you know what was going on. Your son is stable and they are checking for internal bleeding, broken bones and other concerns. While your husband rode with him in the ambulance and since arriving with him, he has been singing to him, and when the doctors have needed to move your husband or speak with him, your son starts to cry immediately when your husband stops singing. But when the daddy starts singing, your son will stop crying. Your son has not had any pain management administered yet because that would interfere with the doctor's evaluation and exam, since he is too young to explain what is happening to him. But your son does not appear to be in any distress as long as his daddy is singing in his ear. So we have asked him to please keep singing."

Within another twenty or thirty minutes, they had ruled out any broken bones and determined there was no apparent internal bleeding. I was informed Judah would be admitted for further testing and examinations, but I could see him now. I was escorted through the diminishing crowd to my Judah's bedside. I got closer to him and my husband, and I could hear three or four voices singing along with my husband as they worked about the room. "Jesus Loves Me" had become the room anthem!! Oh, what a beautiful sound to hear, the first time I saw my son since the tragedy had occurred. I held his hand and tears streamed down my cheeks, and I looked my son Judah in the face. I could still see a frightened little boy, but he knew Jesus was going to take care of him. Daddy told him so.

In the next hour, we had a police officer show up to fill out an incident report. After answering many questions and letting him do his job, he said off the record that he also had a young son at home. He said that when he got the call, his heart hurt thinking of his own boy. He understood that this was just an accident that could have happened to anyone. But after speaking with us and seeing Judah's countenance, this call that could have turned into a horrific tragedy had the potential to have a good ending. He was encouraged and happy to be heading home to his own family. He and my husband talked. My husband encouraging him to pray with his own family that night!

Over the next several days, it became apparent there would be rough days of recovery ahead. We had many visits from the hospital's head surgeon. Each time he came into the hospital room with an attitude that made it apparent he didn't want to speak. (Just let him do his job.) However, on his last visit towards the end of Judah's stay at the hospital, the doctor stated, "You probably thought you saw something happen that didn't."

I was shocked but replied that I would be willing to wake my son up for him to exam the marks still on his body. I reminded him of the ER report stating, "The tire tracks indicated."

The head surgeon commented, "But Ma'am, that would be the equivalent of someone running over a tin can and it not crushing."

I was speechless. The only response I could come up with was, "But I have a good God!"

Andrew: The days to come were such a blur. I don't even remember when they transferred Judah from the ER to his own room in the hospital. My wife and I both tried to get each other to get some rest, but sleep evaded us. It was a few days before they were able to rule out any major organ damage. I could see the heaviness on my wife's face, since she had lost her mother from kidney failure less than a year before. Days turned into a whole week. We were ecstatic when they took all the tubes out of Judah and then took him out of the bed for the first time to see if he could stand. It was exciting, yet so disheartening! This little boy, who before this traumatic event, had been able to keep up with his five-year-old "big" brother, was taking steps as though they were his first, dragging a foot and walking very stiff-legged. I thought to God, "Lord, will Judah ever be able to run again?" God has a way of showing us His power and glory even when we think things will never be the same again.

Just weeks later, when we took our boys to the park, Judah began to walk around the circular walkway surrounding the playground by himself. It was as if a light went on, looking at his face, as he started to make multiple laps running. To this day, Judah shows no sign of scars, or physical handicap. He was even clocked at running a dash within .5 seconds behind his big brother last year. He enjoys basketball, rock climbing, and riding his bike. In church, he is "Our Worshipper!" (In fulfillment of his name.)

Tamara: Judah needed physical therapy. But our God has been so faithful to Judah. By the end of thirty days, we took Judah and our other son, Jaguar, to the park. Judah loved being outside but had not played much since it was a struggle to walk after the accident. But I will never forget that day, as my husband and I stood in the middle of the playground with tears coming down our cheeks. We watched our Judah walk slowly around the playground's sidewalk, following the circle around and around until eventually he walked faster, gaining strength to shift into a run. For about twenty minutes he ran the circular sidewalk. Others standing around would stop and watch while we told them the story of Judah's miracle.

God took the pain and fear and replaced it with praise in my Judah. To this day, he is sometimes the first to run in a church service. Or jumps the highest or sings the loudest. The first song he learned to play on the piano for a church special was, "Jesus Loves Me." I thank God daily for His undeniable healing power! Judah has no scars – no residual effects – no complications – no indications of the event. But he knows that God healed him, and he is a miracle! Through this testimony, God has placed people in our lives whom we have been able to reach with this precious gospel.

People have asked me many times, what would I recount as the most significant part of our son's story? The element with the most significant impact on my life would be the revelation of the importance of investing and instilling the Name of Jesus in our boys' hearts and lives. To bring peace in the midst of storms, to bring joy in place of mourning.

Rev. J. Andrew & Tamara Goodwin

Contac information for speaking engagements:
Revjagoodwin@gmail.com

Diana Cardenas

Conference Speaker

Diana Ministering

Diana & Guillermo Cardenas

CHAPTER 10

Diana Cardenas

"And blessed is he who is not offended because of Me."
Matthew 11:6

P ain has its purpose.

The word pain...no one likes it or wants to talk about it. Success is a key word in today's circles of ministry people. Yet, have we ever considered that some have been chosen for pain? Even failure...a very scary thought for many. You see, there's a difference from being called and being chosen.

"For many are called, but few are chosen."
Matthew 22:14

I've come to understand that when someone is "called," they have a choice to answer or not. Many have been called and have never answered. But when someone has been chosen, there are no options. You have to answer...

> *"I knew you before I formed you in your mother's womb. Before you were born, I set you apart and APPOINTED you as my prophet to the nations."*
> Jeremiah 1:5

The key word in this scripture is "appointed," which according to the Cambridge dictionary means "Officially Chosen." Other definitions are: decided beforehand, preordained, decided, determined and again "chosen."

In other words, it's already been decided.

There's really no way out. Out of what? The process of being chosen and the process of the anointing. Anointing can only come through brokenness and there is no other way around it. Every prophetic word, promise, and calling that the Lord has placed over us comes through a process. All with the purpose of the Lord being able to answer this question: Can He trust you with what He wants to give you? Can He trust you with how He wants to use you? Can He trust you with what belongs to HIM?

Humility can only come through a process of understanding from where and Whom all things come ...Jesus.

It is when you are in the middle of the process of pain, hurting, waiting, not understanding so many things, and maybe never will. Knowing the promises of God over your life, but you've been chosen to wait and chosen to hurt. A decision has to be made that while in the middle of the process, you will still trust the Lord, knowing that you really are in the hands of the Potter, and even though your flesh cries out and the pain of waiting is so profound, yet your heart and spirit say, "I STILL BELEIVE."

"Blessed is she who has believed that The Lord would fulfill His promises to her!" Luke 1:45

To be anointed, you must go through pain, but to be used of God, you must be healed from that pain...healed from the wounds of your suffering. The Lord's healing will give you a testimony and authority over that which He has healed.

BROKEN AT BIRTH:

I am a byproduct of divorce. My parents were married in an Apostolic church by one of the great pioneers of our organization. I'm not sure when it happened, but some time before or soon after I was born, my father fell from God's grace and committed adultery. Most may not share something like this, but it's part of my story and part of my testimony of who I am in God. It's part of my process. My father's sin resulted in divorce between my parents, making my mother a young, beautiful, single mother in the early church. Unfortunately, the church at that time was not prepared or equipped to receive or minister to my mother and me. After trying to serve God and remain faithful, my mother received so much rejection that she ultimately made a decision to not try anymore. This decision caused a spiral effect in different areas of my life. For one, my mother remarried and started a new life without the church. My grandparents took this little girl in and raised me. To this day, I am thankful and understand that it was by God's grace that this happened. I understand that He knew me even before I was born and had chosen a covering over me that would protect and keep me from the snares of the enemy.

Although protected by my grandparents, the divorce and rejection affected certain areas of my life. I was a child with so many complexities, insecurities and low self-esteem issues. I remember not thinking very much of myself and always had a "the least of these" mentality. As I grew, I carried all these complexities with me everywhere I went. It most likely did not show on the outside, but it was all living inside of me. I was a shy little girl, very introverted, rarely spoke, did not look people in their eyes, and usually walked with my head down. For some reason, I always felt shame and embarrassment. Yet, something I never understood back then was that I always felt different and never part of the crowd. There was always something inside of me that knew there was a God and He walked with me.

At the age of twelve, I received the gift of the Holy Ghost and was baptized in the name of Jesus. I will never forget coming out of the waters and feeling so light, as if I was walking on clouds. My life had changed, and life in the Lord was beautiful. But the insecurities still lived inside me.

When I met my husband, who was a deacon at the time and eventually ordained into the ministry, I was still broken and didn't even know it. I took all my insecurities, complexes and low self-esteem issues into my marriage. All these issues affected every area of my life, including my marriage and ministry. Yet, I was called, and more than that, I was chosen.

THE BEGINNING OF MY HEALING:

I remember one Sunday after my husband had preached a powerful message. I was at the altar, complaining to the Lord that I never had a father because he left me. I began to ask the Lord "why this and why that?" I was literally having a pity party and thought the Lord was going to embrace me and tell me I had a reason to be so lowly and poor in spirit. But that was not what happened! All of a sudden, I heard the Lord speak to me strongly. The Lord spoke these words to me: "Who do you think is your Father? Who do you think has protected you from things you don't even know about? I have taken care of you and I HAVE LOVED YOU! I AM your FATHER!" At that moment, the tears stopped and all that I was saying and feeling came to a stop! I repented before the Lord for complaining and wanting a faithful earthly father. I had finally realized that the Father I had was the most faithful man who could ever live...my Heavenly Father! Just receiving His words into my spirit healed my heart and spirit from the wound of being fatherless (although, I never was). From that day forward, I never asked or complained about my earthly father again. Instead, I made an appointment with my father to ask him for forgiveness from the hurt I had toward him for so many years. Of course, this was something he did not understand and was very uncomfortable, yet it was something that I needed to do, to set me free. I was healed from the brokenness of wrong decisions made by my father and any generational curse, as later I learned to intervene through intercessory prayer to break anything generational.

This was just the beginning. I took everything that I had inside of me into my marriage and ministry. I was healed from the brokenness of wrong decisions my father made, but I was still a very insecure woman. And not just a woman, but a woman of God; a phrase I never used in regard to myself because of the shame of knowing how complex and insecure I really was inside. I could not see myself the way God saw me.

I remember my husband and I attending a preaching conference and there I was...me and the Lord, together again, alone at an altar. I've come to understand that the process of being chosen includes "divine appointments." Every day of our lives has already been written, including the day of our healing!

The preacher began to minister and speak life. But I will never forget what he said at the altar call: "If you have to scream it out, do it! No one is going to tell you to stop!" I wasn't sure if I should do it or not, because I knew people there at the conference and they knew me. The pride of being so human can literally take away a divine moment with God. But my desperation was so great that I felt I was about to explode. I told The Lord, "I don't care who's here and if they know me or what they might say, I want to be healed!"

And that was when I opened my mouth! Honestly, there were no words that could express the many years of pain inside me. Where would I even begin? So I did as the preacher said...I didn't care who was around me or who heard me, and I opened my mouth. I literally felt as if an ocean of all that was inside me was just flowing out. I don't know how long I was at the altar. Time elapsed as the Lord was healing and me from every complexity, insecurity, and even anger. When I got up from the altar, my husband had been there the whole time praying with me and was there to help me up. As I looked, there were only a few people left in the sanctuary. The service had ended and everyone had left.

As I walked with my husband, I noticed something different. I noticed the lights in the church, and I wasn't looking at the carpet. I was looking up. As I went into the dining hall where everyone was eating, I noticed that I was looking each person in the eye, with a smile on my face. I noticed the joy I felt, and I noticed that I was not the same person. I felt cleansed. As time went on, I noticed that I loved to laugh and laugh loud! I noticed that my head was up and not down anymore. And when someone would look at me, I would return the look, eye to eye. I learned to look into the eyes of others with discernment, understanding, and knowing that the God who healed me can also heal others.

I was healed.

THE CALL:

"I knew you before I formed you in your mother's womb. Before you were born, I set you apart and appointed you as my prophet to the nations."
Jeremiah 1:5

My husband and I received our first call to the pastorate in 1992, where we pastored a small church in Loma Linda, CA. After serving there for a few years, we were asked to receive the church in San Jacinto, CA. This was a very blessed and prosperous time in our ministry. The

Lord had blessed us with a brand-new home and new furniture. We were blessed financially, we pastored a wonderful church, and there was growth and unity. My husband had just enrolled in school with the intent of finishing his college education. Suddenly, the Lord began to deal with and impress on my husband a calling over his life. He would leave the house and drive to work, school and back home crying. He became very emotional and did not know why. One day, he just surrendered to the Lord and said, "Lord, whatever You want me to do or wherever You want me to go, I surrender." My husband never shared this with anyone and just continued in prayer.

A few months later, we were attending a national convention for our organization. As my husband attended pastoral meetings, the presiding president at that time approached my husband and spoke these words to him: "The mission field is calling, are you ready?... I have just placed the mantle over you." Then he walked away.

I remember after service at dinner, my husband shared what had happened and the words of the president. I was in shock, my children began to cry, and fear entered my heart. There was complete silence at the table. I don't think we knew how to process in our minds such a great calling. All I remember through the years was hearing and seeing our missionaries when they would visit the US. I remember hearing their testimonies of suffering and of great victories in the Lord. There was always admiration and great respect for these men and women of God. But us? I never imagined that the Lord had heard the prayer of a little girl who secretly prayed and desired to help others in a foreign country. I never thought when my husband would express the same desire as a young married couple that God was actually listening. I just never thought...and I was terrified of it.

After that night, we did not speak of the incident again and my husband just continued in prayer.

My fear was so great that one day, standing in my kitchen as I washed dishes, I told the Lord, "No." I remember telling the Lord that I was afraid for my children, and I was barely learning to be a pastor's wife. I didn't even know how to sing and all missionary wives sing! I stood in my kitchen and said no to the Lord. Yet, my "no" was not out of rebellion, but out of so much fear. I did my best to forget about the topic and never brought it up to my husband again.

ANSWERING THE CALL:

A few months later, my husband and I attended a preaching conference in Central California. We went with the intent of being refreshed in spirit and thought it would be a great getaway. We left our children with family and took a road trip to the conference, just the two of us. As the conference began, the Lord started speaking and ministering to us. One of the keynote speakers and the vessel the Lord used was Evangelist George Pantages. He began his sermon, "When I Said Yes," and I remember hearing his testimony of becoming an evangelist, all his personal insecurities, language barriers, etc., and it really caught my attention. At one point he said these words: "You're afraid! Afraid for your children and what might happen to them. The Lord will take care of you and your children! Don't be afraid!" At that moment, I remembered my "no" to the Lord that day in my kitchen. My "no" was out of fear for my children and the unknown. While Bro.

Pantages continued to preach, I felt as if I was the only person in the church. I felt as if he was pointing to me and speaking directly to me, as if everyone around me had disappeared. It felt like an audience of one with just me and the Lord. I went to the altar after the preaching and broke before the Lord. I asked God for forgiveness for saying "no" to Him. I was so broken that I don't even think I understood what was really happening. All I could do was cry and cry. I cried so much that I was literally a mess from wiping and wiping away my tears. I surrendered and whispered, "Yes" to the Lord that day at that altar. The Lord had healed all my fears.

    I was still at the altar when the next preacher got up to begin his sermon. The preacher was Bishop Julian Aguirre, and he began with these words: "I came prepared to preach another sermon, but the Lord just changed it because there is a couple here that the Lord is calling to the mission field!"

    At this point, I was not only completely surrendered, but I was convinced that the Lord had chosen us and placed the call over our lives to the mission field. This was it! And I knew it!

    I managed to get through the next sermon about missions, but I was left completely exhausted from so much crying and surrendering. That same night at the last service, there was one last altar call. My husband looked at me to go up with him, but I couldn't out of pure exhaustion. I was so weak and tired from the Lord dealing with me, I couldn't take it anymore. I told my husband to go up and whatever the Lord told him, just tell me and I would receive it.

As my husband was praying at the altar, Evangelist Pantages gave my husband a word, "The Lord is calling you to the mission field!"

THE VISION:

We made our way home with a new perspective and understanding of what the Lord was doing in our lives. Nonetheless, we still needed to speak to our children, with the hopes that they would receive the news well. We purchased the recorded preachings for our children to hear as usual. As our two older children, Wille and Vanessa began to hear the preachings, the Lord spoke directly to them. One day as I was in the kitchen, our son walked in and said, "Mom, the Lord is calling us to the mission field." We began to seek counsel and instruction as to the next steps to take with our authorities. My husband continued in prayer, taking our children before the Lord for more confirmation. One night as we were sleeping, my husband was awakened by a voice calling his name. As he woke up, he could see the form of a man standing at the foot of our bed. He could not see facial features or any other detail, only his form. The man told him to get up and read Genesis 13:13 and beyond. At that moment, the man disappeared. My husband immediately got up and read the scripture: Genesis 13:13-18

Now the people of Sodom were wicked and were sinning greatly against the Lord. The Lord said to Abram after Lot had parted from him, "Look around from where you are, to the north and south, to the east and west. All the land that you see I will give to you and your offspring forever. I will make your offspring like the dust of the earth, so that if anyone could count the dust, then your offspring could be counted. Go, walk through the length and breadth of the land, for I am giving it to you." So Abram went to live near the great trees of Mamre at Hebron, where he pitched his tents. There he built an altar to the Lord.

This was the confirmation that my husband needed. One year later, we found ourselves driving to the country of Canada to serve as missionaries.

THE PAIN OF THE CALL: BROKENNESS

As we arrived at our new home and our new country, we were overwhelmed with joy and shock. The joy of the Lord for this new season, and the shock of leaving all behind and entering the unknown. I never forgot the words of the preacher, "The Lord does not call us because we are so experienced and know so much, He calls us to show us so much more!" As we began to pastor and supervise the work of the Lord in Canada, the Lord began to bless and prosper His church. Eight months after arriving, the Lord blessed His church with the purchase of a sanctuary and pastoral home. The previous missionaries, Ruben and Lydia Bernal, had worked very hard together with the congregation in London, Ontario, to raise funds with the goal and dream of purchasing the first church property for the country after ten years of being established. The church was joyful and rejoicing for all that God was doing. An Inauguration service was planned and prepared with great anticipation, as our leaders and authorities would be coming from the US to celebrate this victory. The service was beautiful and the Lord blessed His church at this historical event.

The next day after all the festivities and all had returned to the US, our family decided to take a day off and take our children to eat at a restaurant, which is a treat for missionary children. As we were enjoying our day off and everything seemed normal, as we were eating dinner, I all of a sudden began to feel very sick. My heart began to pound in my chest, I felt lightheaded, I broke into a cold sweat, I felt as if I was going to pass out, and I couldn't breathe. By the grace of God, I had always been healthy and had really never experienced any kind of sickness before in my life! I did not know what was happening to me. The restaurant called 911 and the paramedics came to attend to me. I thought I was having a heart attack and the paramedics did not know what or why I had these symptoms. They rushed me to the hospital and many tests were done. The doctors could not find anything wrong with me and sent me home.

About one week after that incident, I was at home by myself with my two younger girls. All of a sudden, the same symptoms began all over again. I became so weak that I fell on the sofa and just lay there, unable to move. The paramedics came and rushed me to the hospital again. But this time I noticed something different...the moment they pushed me through the double doors of the emergency department, the symptoms stopped! They did all the same tests and could find nothing physically wrong with me. The weeks following, I had several episodes with the same symptoms, going back and forth to the hospital. These episodes were taking a toll on my body and I became physically weaker and weaker. I didn't understand what was happening with me and I began to cry out unto the Lord. All I knew was that I was very weak, and at times I would just drop to the floor when the symptoms began. I would find myself again either being taken to the hospital or my family surrounding me as they prayed. All I could do was surrender myself to whatever was happening.

This was the beginning and onset of a deep depression and anxiety that attacked my mind and body. The doctors ruled out any other possibilities and diagnosed me with having panic attacks. Panic attacks! I had never heard of such a thing, and all I knew was that I felt like I was having a heart attack, and every time I had the symptoms I felt like I was dying. Every attack left me weaker and weaker. The depression progressed to the point that I could not sleep and experienced insomnia. If I did get any sleep, it would be at the most twenty to thirty minutes a night! While my family slept peacefully throughout the nights, I would spend my nights on the floor of my bedroom, crying out to the Lord! I would ask Him to have mercy on me and to heal me! The body needs sleep, and when it doesn't get it, it begins to shut down. I remember having no feeling, and just emotional numbness. I couldn't focus or think straight. I stopped taking care of my family, I stopped cooking, cleaning, and one day while trying to put a load of clothes in the washer, I couldn't remember how to separate colors from whites. Another day as I ironed my husband's shirts, I forgot to iron the other half of the shirt and didn't notice until I handed it to him. One day taking the kids to a fast food place, I couldn't focus enough to order a simple meal for my kids and broke down crying in front of the cashier. I couldn't do the simple everyday things anymore. The lack of sleep had taken its toll on my body, my mind, emotions, and spirit. Everything about me was weak. There were days when my baby girls would come up to me, seeking my attention, and I wouldn't even look at them because I was so unfocused, and weak. These were dark days for me; days where the enemy would attack my mind and try to make me think that I was going to die.

It got to the point where my oldest daughter had to step in and start cooking, cleaning, and taking care of the two youngest girls. I stopped eating and was losing a lot of weight. It got so bad that my husband had to remind me to eat, and I remember one time he actually spoon-fed me. This all caused stress on everyone in my home. I remember my kids fighting with each other because of all the pressure my state of being was causing. I just sat in the living room crying as I witnessed the toll it was taking on my family. There were moments when the panic attacks were so severe, I would throw myself on the floor and just cry out to God for mercy. My husband and children couldn't recognize me anymore. I remember my husband saying, "I just want my wife back!"

The nights were the worst, and I would dread the sun going down. I remember the enemy coming to me at night and telling me, "You left everything for your God only for Him to bring you here to die! You're going back home in a coffin! All for your God!"

I had never experienced this type of spiritual warfare in my life! The enemy would go full force and attack my mind with so many lies. I began to study God's Word, and for the first time understood fully what spiritual warfare was about and that it was real. And for the first time I was in full brokenness of spirit, body and mind. All of me was weak and broken. I was at the bottom with nowhere else to look but up. I sought God for the answers, and I would pray and pray. Prayer was all I had. This was a brokenness that I had no control over. I did not know where this was leading, and I didn't know how to make it go away.

All this was happening to me, my husband, my family and my home, while we were missionaries, pastors and supervisors of a country. How could that be? And why would the Lord allow such ugliness in my life? What did I do wrong? This was a question I would ask the Lord so many times. And I would plead His forgiveness, in case there was something I couldn't remember. Yet, the brokenness continued.

I was so desperate to hear from God! One day another missionary, a man of God called me from the other side of the world. Bishop Joe Prado called to tell me that the Lord had shown him what I was going through. This man of God, together with his wife, Sis. Patty Prado, prayed for me and walked me through what was happening in my life. Bro. Prado prophesied over me and gave me a word from the Lord: "One day you will minister to many women!" I received that word and I believed it with all my heart! But in the middle of my brokenness and pain, I couldn't even begin to try to understand what the word meant or think about when it would happen. All I wanted was my healing!

One night as my family slept and I was there on the floor praying, the enemy came as he always did at night to tell me the same thing. "You left everything for your God, only to come here and die!" I don't know how, but I gathered all the energy I had and finally answered! I decided to talk back and rebuke the enemy and said, "Well, if I die, I die! But the Lord called me here and I will do and finish what He has asked me to do!"

All of a sudden, something inside of me rose up! A fight! A fight to believe God and not the enemy! Every day was a struggle. Sometimes I had good days, and sometimes I had bad days. And all I had was prayer, His Word, a promise and some faith to STILL BELIEVE.

THE POTTER'S HOUSE:

There was a potter's house a few miles from our home in Canada and on one of my "bad" days, my husband decided to take me there. It was a very beautiful and serene place with a lake in the middle of the property. There were two buildings on the property, the potter's house and a gift shop where they sold all the pottery made there by hand. When we arrived, the potter was preparing to make a vessel and was kind enough to show us the process. He shared with my husband and me that before he places the clay on the wheel, he must first work the clay with his hands and pound it against a cold cement table to get the air bubbles out of it. As the potter placed a clump of clay on the wheel, he began to form a vessel. We watched in amazement and awe to actually witness a vessel being formed in front of our eyes. I remember feeling so humbled, and a sense of purpose in the room. I could feel the fear of the Lord in my spirit because I knew the Lord had a message for me. As we watched the potter working the clay and forming the vessel on the wheel, I noticed how dirty his hands were. I noticed the sharp instruments he was using to carve and cut into the clay. The whole time I was thinking, "Is this what You are doing to me, Lord?" As the potter cut excess clay from the vessel, I could almost feel its pain. I felt so overwhelmed by what I was seeing, I just wanted to run out of that potter's house and cry out to God. And yet, I could hear the Lord tell me, "That's you." As the potter continued to form the vessel, all of a sudden, with no warning, the potter crushed and marred the beautiful vessel! He crushed the vessel that he had been working on and was almost finished! My husband and I looked at each other with shock and asked the potter why did he do that?

The potter said, "I crushed it because as I was working the vessel, I could feel air bubbles with my fingers." He went on to explain that the air bubbles were too tiny to be seen by the human eye, but he could feel them with his fingers. Of course, we asked him what he was going to do with the marred vessel...his answer was to return it and restart the process all over again. My husband became intrigued with what we were witnessing and asked what would have happened if he would have allowed the vessel to continue the process. The potter explained that if he would have allowed the vessel to continue the process into the oven, as the heat began to rise, the vessel would have exploded during intense fire and its particles would have pierced and destroy the other vessels around it!

I can't tell you what that day at the potter's house did to me! It humbled me, it spoke to me, and the Lord opened my eyes to understand that I was a vessel on the Potter's wheel.

Jeremiah 18:1-6

This is the word that came to Jeremiah from the Lord: "Go down to the potter's house, and there I will give you my message." So I went down to the potter's house, and I saw him working at the wheel. But the pot he was shaping from the clay was marred in his hands; so the potter formed it into another pot, shaping it as seemed best to him.

Then the word of the Lord came to me. He said, "Can I not do with you, Israel, as this potter does?" declares the Lord. "Like clay in the hand of the potter, so are you in my hand, Israel."

The Lord used the potter's house experience to reveal to me what He was doing in my life. I was broken, I was being attacked, I was weak, depressed, hurting, humbled, and I was being formed by the Master Potter. I had decided to allow myself to be on the Potter's wheel fully surrendered. My healing was a process, but it was all according to God's perfect will.

Yes, healing comes when He chooses for it to come. When He has accomplished a work in you. And even then, that work will still need to be perfected. Yet, one thing is for sure...

"I will not die, but live, and proclaim what The Lord has done!" Psalm 118:17

God has kept His promise over my life. I've had to trust and believe God. I never imagined where my process was taking me, but it was more than I could ever think in my mind. I've seen the Lord heal physically, emotionally, mentally, and restore and liberate His daughters. My pain has taken me to a place in God and life that I never thought possible. I've come to understand the cost of the anointing, but more importantly, the responsibility of keeping it. I've learned to still BELIEVE.

"Blessed is she who has believed that The Lord would fulfill His Promises to her!" Luke 1:45

The Lord chooses to use broken vessels. He uses vessels that are familiar with pain and understand that pain has its purpose. He uses vessels that have seen the hand of God over their lives. Vessels that have been broken and healed.

Yes, God can use you...

Contac information for speaking engagements:
Dianacardenas6583@gmail.com

"Thanks for reading! If you enjoyed this book or found it useful I'd be very grateful if you'd post a short review on Amazon. Your support really does make a difference and I read all the reviews personally so I can get your feedback and make my books even better.

Thanks again for your support!"

George Pantages Ministries

Books Available in English

George Pantages Ministries
Cell 512-785-6324
GEOPANJR@YAHOO.COM
GEORGEPANTAGES.COM

GEORGE PANTAGES MINISTRIES

LIBROS DISPONIBLES EN ESPAÑOL

GEORGE PANTAGES MINISTRIES
CELL 512-785-6324
GEOPANJR@YAHOO.COM
GEORGEPANTAGES.COM

www.ingramcontent.com/pod-product-compliance
Lightning Source LLC
LaVergne TN
LVHW051605070426
835507LV00021B/2777